Green Finance and Investment

Measuring Green Finance Flows in Kazakhstan

This work is published under the responsibility of the Secretary-General of the OECD. The opinions expressed and arguments employed herein do not necessarily reflect the official views of OECD member countries.

This document, as well as any data and map included herein, are without prejudice to the status of or sovereignty over any territory, to the delimitation of international frontiers and boundaries and to the name of any territory, city or area.

Please cite this publication as:
OECD (2020), *Measuring Green Finance Flows in Kazakhstan*, Green Finance and Investment, OECD Publishing, Paris, *https://doi.org/10.1787/3ef6618c-en*.

ISBN 978-92-64-55522-8 (print)
ISBN 978-92-64-31676-8 (pdf)

Green Finance and Investment
ISSN 2409-0336 (print)
ISSN 2409-0344 (online)

Photo credits: Cover © mika48/Shutterstock.com.

Corrigenda to publications may be found on line at: *www.oecd.org/about/publishing/corrigenda.htm*.
© OECD 2020

The use of this work, whether digital or print, is governed by the Terms and Conditions to be found at *http://www.oecd.org/termsandconditions*.

Foreword

The Committee on Statistics of the Ministry of National Economy of Kazakhstan has been working on the quantitative and qualitative indicators that monitor progress towards the country's green economy transition. Using the OECD methodology on Green Growth Indicators (GGIs), the committee has identified 38 country-specific GGIs. The indicators include those on environmental protection expenditures and foreign direct investment related to green growth.

This report explores how Kazakhstan's national statistical system can be further improved. These enhancements could lead to better measurement of the financial flows that contribute to the country's green economy transition. At the same time, they would minimise the risk of creating an undue reporting burden on the private and public sector.

This report was drafted by Takayoshi Kato (OECD). Kumi Kitamori and Krzysztof Michalak (OECD) provided overall guidance. The author thanks Assel Shauenova (the Committee on Statistics), Aliya Shalabekova (the Ministry of Ecology, Geology and Natural Resources) and Aday Nygmanov (JSC Center for the Development of Trade Policy) for their thorough support in the implementation of this project, and Mireille Martini (OECD) for her contribution of Annex 3. The author is grateful for intellectual input provided by various institutions of the government of Kazakhstan: the Committee on Statistics under the Ministry of National Economy; the Ministry of Ecology, Geology and Natural Resources; and JSC Center for the Development of Trade Policy, as well as the Astana International Financial Centre. The report also greatly benefited from expert review and valuable input from colleagues at the OECD Secretariat: Alexander Dobrinevski, Guy Halpern, Raphaël Jachnik, Jean-François Lengelle, Krzysztof Michalak, Alexandre Martoussevitch and Nelly Petkova. The author also appreciates invaluable insights provided by Florian Flachenecker (European Commission Joint Research Centre), Myriam Linster (OECD) and Andrei Isac. Maria Dubois and Mark Foss also supported the author with the publication process.

This work was financially supported by the German Federal Ministry for the Environment, Nature Conservation and Nuclear Safety, and implemented under the GREEN Action Task Force hosted by the OECD.

Table of contents

Foreword 3

Abbreviations and acronyms 7

Executive summary 9
    Recommendations 9

1 Understanding financial flows for Kazakhstan's green economy transition 11
    Developing policies for green economy transition 12
    Objectives of this study 12
    Understanding financial needs for green economy transition 14
    References 16
    Notes 17

2 Statistics on environmental expenditures in Kazakhstan: Current state of affairs 19
    What kind of green finance is measured in Kazakhstan? 20
    How does Kazakhstan's national statistical system collect data? 23
    What figures do the available data sets show? 25
    Annex 2.A. Full data on current and investment expenditures for environmental protection by sector and by CEPA class 38
    Annex 2.B. Work by the Committee on Statistics 40
    References 42
    Notes 43

3 Informing further development: International initiatives on measuring financial flows for green economy 45
    Context 46
    Existing and upcoming initiatives that can inform regular measurement of green finance flows in Kazakhstan 47
    Implications for further improvement in Kazakhstan's national statistical system 55
    Annex 3.A. The European Commission's Action Plan on Financing Sustainable Growth 56
    References 57
    Notes 60

FIGURES

Figure 2.1. Conceptual link between measurement of green finance and Kazakhstan's current statistical system on environmental and green economy expenditures 21

Figure 2.2. Trends in environmental expenses provided by Kazakh entities for environmental protection (excluding investment expenditures) 24
Figure 2.3. Investment and current expenditure for environmental protection as share of GDP 27
Figure 2.4. Availability of disaggregated data on current expenditure of environmental protection 28
Figure 2.5. Current environmental expenditures (current costs only) by region 29
Figure 2.6. Trends in current expenditure for environmental protection (current costs only) 30
Figure 2.7. Top six industries spending current expenditures for environmental protection 31
Figure 2.8. Availability of disaggregated data on investment expenditure of environmental protection 32
Figure 2.9. Investment expenditures in environmental protection 33
Figure 2.10. Investment environmental expenditures by region 34
Figure 2.11. Top six industries spending investment expenditures for environmental protection and their purposes by CEPA class 36

TABLES

Table 1.1. Investment needs for implementation of the 2013 Concept on Transition to Green Economy 15
Table 2.1. Summary of definitions of expenditures for environmental protection and resource management 22
Table 2.2. Different sources and state of tracking 25
Table 2.3. Investment and current expenditures of environmental protection and certain resource management activities from 2015 to 2017 26
Table 2.4. Investment expenditures for environmental protection by activity 33
Table 2.5. Investment expenditure for "green economy" related activities 37
Table 3.1. Selected standards and classifications and their possible contributions to improving methodologies to measure green finance in Kazakhstan 47
Table 3.2. Classes under CReMA and examples of activities 49
Table 3.3. Examples of climate change mitigation and adaptation activities 51

Annex Table 2.A.1. Current expenditures for environmental protection by sector and by CEPA class 38
Annex Table 2.A.2. Investment expenditures for environmental protection by sector and by CEPA class 39

Abbreviations and acronyms

AIFC	Astana International Financial Centre
CEPA	Classification of Environmental Protection Activities
CPEIR	Climate Public Expenditures and Institutional Review
CReMA	Classification of Resource Management Activities
CRS	Creditor Reporting System
EC	European Commission
EGSS	Environmental Goods and Services Sector
EPEA	Environmental Protection Expenditure Accounts
EPER	Environmental Protection Expenditure and Revenues
Eurostat	European Statistical Office
FDI	foreign direct investment
GDP	gross domestic product
GGI	Green Growth Indicator
GHG	greenhouse gas
GRP	gross regional product
HLEG	High-Level Expert Group
KZT	Kazakh Tenge
SEEA	System of Environmental-Economic Accounts
TEG	Technical Expert Group
UNDP	United Nations Development Programme
USD	US Dollar
WPEI	Working Party on Environmental Information

Executive summary

Credible statistical information can serve as a powerful tool for the Republic of Kazakhstan (Kazakhstan) to plan for, and monitor progress on, its transition to a green economy. The government of Kazakhstan, particularly the Committee on Statistics under the Ministry of National Economy, has been working on the quantitative and qualitative characteristics of indicators related to the country's green economy transition. Those indicators include information on investment and current (or operational) expenditures for environmental protection activities.

This report examines how Kazakhstan can further improve its national statistical system to better measure and understand financial flows that contribute to the country's green economy transition. It attempts to answer multiple research questions to identify approaches for the regular measurement of green finance flows within Kazakhstan:

- How does the statistical system work in Kazakhstan?
- What does the available data show us about green finance flows?
- How can the statistical system be improved so it can better measure green finance flows, while minimising the risk of creating an undue reporting burden?
- How can a range of relevant international and national initiatives on sustainable finance help Kazakhstan improve the statistical system?

The Committee on Statistics annually collects and publishes data on environmental expenditures in Kazakhstan, in accordance with the European standard statistical Classification of Environmental Protection Activities (CEPA).

Statistical data show that Kazakh public and private entities spent KZT 87 billion (or USD 230 million) of investment expenditures and KZT 175.4 billion (or USD 462 million) of current (operational) expenditures in 2017. The level of investment and current expenditures for environmental protection as a share of gross domestic product (GDP) remains relatively low, compared to those of the EU countries. Over 2015-2017, investment and current expenditures as shares of GDP are 0.2% on average and 0.4%, respectively.

Based on discussions with the OECD through this study, the Committee on Statistics broadened its data collection on current expenditures. Beyond environmental protection activities, the committee has decided to collect data on current expenditures for energy efficiency, renewable energy and other climate mitigation actions. Until 2019, these three types of expenditures had been collected for investment expenditures for these activities, but not for current expenditures.

Recommendations

Make further disaggregated data available to inform policy-making

Kazakhstan can publish data on expenditures for environmental protection and resource management disaggregated by entity in the public sector (e.g. major ministries, state-owned enterprises and other public bodies engaged in environmental protection and green economy activities). While each ministry's budget-related documents may contain some disaggregated data, it would be useful to make them publicly available in one place (e.g. an annual statistical report by the Committee on Statistics). This could provide policy makers with a more comprehensive account of financial sources and flows for actions towards green economy.

Improve the statistical system through greater alignment with other methods

Available data do not distinguish between expenditures made by businesses, governments and households. In addition, the statistical system does not break expenditures down into services specific to environmental protection, connected products, adapted goods and capital formation. The Committee on Statistics should continue efforts to further improve the national statistical system based on the System of Environmental-Economic Accounts (SEEA), CEPA and Green Growth Indicators.

Expand data collection to cover other key activities

The Committee on Statistics can also expand the data collection on activities for which current and investment expenditures are measured. Examples of activities that are not covered in the existing system include water resource management, use of forest resources and climate change adaptation. Expanding the scope of collection could identify major investment gaps and possible policy options to bridge these gaps. In this way, the system could help meet the country's targets for green economy transition.

Adopt appropriate lessons from others to measure green finance flows

Various international- and national-level initiatives can help the Committee on Statistics further elaborate principles, metrics and criteria for measuring green finance flows within the country. These initiatives include the European Union's Taxonomy on Sustainable Economic Activities, the European Classification of Resource Management Activities (CReMA), the OECD Environmental Protection Expenditures and Revenues (EPER), the Research Collaborative on Tracking Finance for Climate Action, and the Climate Public Expenditures and Institutional Review (CPEIR), among others.

Measure public spending on environmentally beneficial subsidies

Measuring public spending on environmentally beneficial subsidies could help complement the landscape of green finance flows in Kazakhstan. The Committee on Statistics could collect data on, for instance, subsidies related to renewable energy provided under the Kazakh law "On support for the use of renewable energy sources", record the data as green finance, and report them under the SEEA.

Use enhanced information on green finance for more granular policy analysis

More precise, comprehensive and timely measurement of green finance in Kazakhstan would help the government promote policy discussion on green economy transition on various fronts. This would include identifying sectors, sub-sectors or geographical areas where gaps between investment needs and spending are particularly large; providing evidence base for discussion on factors that promote or inhibit green finance mobilisation; assessing effectiveness of policy or financial interventions; and developing and adopting a variety of financial instruments for green economy transition.

Deepen co-operation among ministries and agencies within Kazakhstan

Greater co-operation between the Committee on Statistics and other ministries and agencies is also of utmost importance. Such agencies include the Ministries of Ecology, Energy, Finance, Industry and Infrastructure Development, and National Economy, as well as the National Bank of the Republic of Kazakhstan. Enhanced collaboration could allow for a greater level of data availability and quality, such as on foreign direct investment directed to activities that can promote Kazakhstan's green economy transition.

1 Understanding financial flows for Kazakhstan's green economy transition

This chapter recaps recent economic developments in Kazakhstan on its transition to a green economy. This includes new and amended environmental policies adopted since independence, as well as other strategic documents. It identifies the objectives of this report, including three research questions to move the country towards more robust and comprehensive regular measurement of green finance flows. It estimates investment needs for achieving such a green transition. This leads to discussion on why Kazakhstan should measure green finance flows and improve its statistical system for this purpose. The chapter also identifies important sources of finance that are excluded from the report, while recognising the need for future work to capture them.

Developing policies for green economy transition

The Republic of Kazakhstan (Kazakhstan), a land-locked country with the ninth largest land area in the world, has made remarkable economic progress since its independence. In 2006, Kazakhstan moved from a lower middle-income to an upper middle-income country. The global financial crisis of 2008 had a sharp, but brief, effect on the country's economy. In 2010 and 2011, its gross domestic product (GDP) grew by 7.3% and 7.4% respectively, a growth rate that remained stable until 2013. More than half of the country's export income is related to the hydrocarbon industry (US Department of Commerce, 2018[1]). This makes the economy highly dependent on world oil prices. In 2014, mainly due to the decline in international commodity prices, GDP growth started to decline, dropping to 1.2% in 2015 and then to 1.1% in 2016. GDP growth recovered in 2017 to 4.1% and continued at a similar level in 2018. The recovery from the 2014-16 collapse in oil prices in Kazakhstan has been supported by higher than expected production in the Kashagan oil field and strong domestic demand (World Bank, 2019[2]).

Kazakhstan has consistently developed new and amended environmental policies since its independence. The key environmental legislative acts in Kazakhstan, specified in the 2007 Environmental Code[1], were amended 62 times between 2007-17 (UNECE, 2019[3]). Among other reasons, these amendments sought inclusion of the regulation and assessment of greenhouse gas (GHG) emissions and capture, waste management and environmental audit, and more recently, better compliance with the polluter pays principle (UNECE, 2019[3]).

Kazakhstan has also adopted various strategic documents on sustainable development and transition to a green economy. The Message of the President on 14 December 2012 delivered a national-level strategy, Kazakhstan-2050, as the key development vision of the country. The strategy establishes, among others, a target for Kazakhstan to become one of the 30 most developed countries by 2050. It also includes the task to make Kazakhstan a global player in environmentally clean agricultural production (UNECE, 2019[3]).

In 2013, the country adopted the Concept on Transition to Green Economy (Green Economy Concept) and its action plan for 2013-20. It provides an important foundation for how Kazakhstan should move forward with its green growth agenda (Government of Kazakhstan, 2013[4]). The priority tasks defined under the Concept span wide areas. These areas include increasing efficiency of resource use, modernising and building infrastructure, improving well-being of the population and environmental quality, and strengthening water security.

The Strategic Plan for Development until 2025, adopted in 2018, also includes the issue of green growth and environmental protection as one of its seven pillars. The strategic plan also includes two indicators on the energy intensity of GDP and the share of renewable energy sources that relate specifically to the country's green economy and environmental protection agenda (UNECE, 2019[3]). All those policy documents explicitly or implicitly indicate the importance of investments in necessary actions on climate change, environmental protection and rational use of natural resources.

Objectives of this study

The Committee on Statistics of the Ministry of National Economy (Committee on Statistics) has been working on the quantitative and qualitative characteristics of indicators to monitor progress towards the country's green economy transition. Kazakhstan's statistical system collects certain information on financial flows, such as investment and current (or operational) expenditures for environmental protection. Various bodies are committed to strengthening the country's statistical system: the Committee on Statistics; the Ministry of Energy; and the Ministry of Ecology, Geology and Natural Resources (as of July 2019, the Ministry of Ecology).

This report examines how Kazakhstan can further improve its national statistical system to better measure and understand financial flows that contribute to the country's green economy transition. These improvements would, at the same time, minimise the risk of creating an undue reporting burden on the private and public sectors. The report examines methodologies for measuring the flows of green finance[2] within Kazakhstan. In so doing, it intends to build on Kazakhstan's national statistical system. This system has been developed in line with the System of Environmental-Economic Accounting (SEEA) and was still in the process of further convergence as of March 2019 (OECD, 2019[5]).

This report attempts to answer multiple research questions to enable robust and comprehensive regular measurement of green finance flows within the country:

- How does the statistical system work in Kazakhstan?
- What do available data show us about green finance?
- What are areas for improved measurement of green finance flows?
- How can a range of relevant international and national finance tracking initiatives help Kazakhstan improve the statistical system?

This report first reviews data collection in Kazakhstan. It analyses the statistics on investment and current (or operational) expenditures for environmental protection, which the Committee on Statistics has already collected and made public. Such an exercise aims to better understand the state of affairs on (part of) green finance flows in Kazakhstan. It also aims to identify possible data gaps and ways to improve collecting, collating and reporting the information.

The report then reviews recent development of various international classifications and methodologies. These provide useful insights and a theoretical basis to enhance the quality and comprehensiveness of statistical information on green finance flows in Kazakhstan. It also reviews definitions of green finance in and outside the country, aiming to clarify reporting expectations on green finance for Kazakh entities. These reviews can inform the country's effort for improving methodologies to measure green finance flows more efficiently. They can also make outcomes of the tracking more relevant to developing policy that supports the country's green economy transition.

Based on the abovementioned analyses, this report recommends ways to strengthen the quality of statistical information related to expenditures for actions towards the country's green economy. Improvement of the statistical system should also be linked to overall policy development by relevant Kazakh ministries on the green economy. Such information may also help the government move towards low-carbon, climate-resilient and environmentally responsible budgeting, as well as an effective monitoring and evaluation system for implemented policies. Indeed, linking expenditures and green economy policy objectives can provide insights into the distribution of resources across these policy objectives, at national and sub-national levels. It may also help identify gaps between resource allocations and investment needs to achieve policy objectives for Kazakhstan's green economy transition (see also, for example, (UNDP, 2015[6])).

This report examines finance flows from republican and local governments, state-owned entities (e.g. Development Bank of Kazakhstan, Damu Fund, Samruk Kazyna), and private-sector entities. Consequently, it excludes some important sources of finance due to its intention to build on the national statistical system, while recognising the need for future analytical work to capture them. First, this report does not discuss foreign direct investments or multilateral and bilateral development finance (public sector) (see Box 1.1). The scope also excludes finance by households and parts of private-sector entities that are currently not recorded on the business registry of Kazakhstan.

> **Box 1.1. Financial flows outside the scope of the study**
>
> Foreign direct investment (FDI) and household spending can be important sources of green finance, but are outside the scope of this study due to unavailability of data. The National Bank of Kazakhstan (the central bank) collects data on FDI. However, to date, FDI data have not been systematically disaggregated between those that target activities for green economy or environmental protection and those that do not. The statistical system does also not collect household expenditures for environmental protection or resource management (e.g. for energy efficiency at residential buildings).
>
> Development finance to Kazakhstan is also not within the scope of this study. However, it is reviewed in an earlier OECD publication (OECD, 2016[7]) and more updated data are also available (OECD DAC, 2018[8]). The OECD Development Assistance Committee's Creditor Reporting System (CRS) publishes annual detailed information from bilateral and multilateral providers of development co-operation on individual activities that target the global environmental objectives (i.e. climate change mitigation and adaptation, biodiversity and desertification) (OECD DAC, 2018[8]). Activity- or project-level data from CRS are available on a commitment base, but not a disbursement (expenditure) base. Some reporting entities registered under the Kazakhstan's business registry may use developing finance for their investments in environmental protection or resource management activities. As such, they may report such finance as environmental protection or resource management expenditures.
>
> Development finance from bilateral and multilateral providers still play an important role in Kazakhstan. This is especially the case for implementing technical assistance projects and catalysing private-sector investments in environmental protection and resource management. Multilateral and bilateral providers of finance have supported such investments by, for instance, reducing project risks, providing seed funding and debt funding, and extending credit lines through local financial institutions.
>
> Sources: (OECD, 2016[7]), https://dx.doi.org/10.1787/9789264266339-en; (OECD DAC, 2018[8]), https://stats.oecd.org/Index.aspx?datasetcode=CRS1.

Understanding financial needs for green economy transition

Finance is a crucial enabler to achieve the targets under key policy documents, such as Kazakhstan's Strategic Plan for Development, and the Green Economy Concept and its action plans. The government recognises that a range of international and domestic financial sources is already delivering "green finance" to, for instance, industry, households and sub-national governments within the country. While there are different definitions of "green finance", in the context of Kazakhstan the term means finance from public and private sources that supports greening of the country's economy. Further, green finance should promote long-term and inclusive economic growth, while avoiding negative impacts of economic activities on communities in Kazakhstan.

Achieving the ambitious targets under the Green Economy Concept is likely to require further scaling-up of such finance from levels in Table 1.1. Using a macroeconomic model, the scale of gross investment needs for implementation of the Concept would be about USD 119.9 billion between 2014 and 2049 (or USD 3.4 billion annually) in 2010 prices Table 1.1 (Government of Kazakhstan, 2013[4]). These estimates are disaggregated into several key sectors covering energy supply and demand, water, air pollution, waste management and efficient agriculture practices. This figure accounts for 1.8% of GDP between 2020-24, and about 1% of GDP for the entire implementation period. The estimate assumes the private sector will provide most of the finance (Government of Kazakhstan, 2013[4]).

Table 1.1. Investment needs for implementation of the 2013 Concept on Transition to Green Economy

	2014-15	2016-17	2018-19	2020-24	2025-29	2030-39	2040-49
Funding needs as percentage of GDP	0.31	0.44	1.23	1.79	0.77	0.59	0.61
Average annual funding needs for period (USD billion in 2010 prices)	0.6	1.0	3.1	5.5	3.0	3.0	3.8
Total over the period (USD billion in 2010 prices)	1.2	2	6.2	27.5	15	30	38

Source: Adapted from (Government of Kazakhstan, 2013[4]), https://www.oneplanetnetwork.org/sites/default/files/kazakhstan_concept_for_transition_of_the_republic_of_kazakhstan_to_green_economy.pdf .

An in-depth analysis of how Kazakh public- and private-sector entities are using financial resources for action on environmental protection, resource management and climate change would provide evidence to identify investment gaps. It could also help the government explore the size of these gaps and how the needed investment could be mobilised for underfunded activities or sectors. Participants in the First Kazakhstan GREEN Action Policy Dialogue held in Astana in 2016 also raised issues related to the information gap (OECD, 2016[9]).

References

Government of Kazakhstan (2013), *CONCEPT for transition of the Republic of Kazakhstan to Green Economy Astana 2013 2 Contents*, approved by Decree of the President of the Republic of Kazakhstan on 20 May 2013 #557, https://www.oneplanetnetwork.org/sites/default/files/kazakhstan_concept_for_transition_of_the_republic_of_kazakhstan_to_green_economy.pdf. [4]

OECD (2019), *Agreement between the government of the Republic of Kazakhstan and the Organisation for Economic Co-operation and Development for the realisation of the project "Implementation of the System of Environmental Economic Accounting": Interim Report*, OECD, Paris. [5]

OECD (2016), *Financing Climate Action in Eastern Europe, the Caucasus and Central Asia*, Green Finance and Investment, OECD Publishing, Paris, https://dx.doi.org/10.1787/9789264266339-en. [7]

OECD (2016), *Kazakhstan GREEN Action Platform*, http://www.oecd.org/env/outreach/kazakhstangreenactionplatform.htm (accessed on 16 January 2019). [9]

OECD DAC (2018), "OECD DAC Creditor Reporting System (CRS) 2018", (database) (Accessed on 08 February 2019), https://stats.oecd.org/Index.aspx?datasetcode=CRS1. [8]

UNDP (2015), *A Methodological Guidebook: Climate Public Expenditure and Institutional Review (CPEIR)*, UNDP Bangkok Regional Hub, http://www.asia-pacific.undp.org/content/rbap/en/home/library/democratic_governance/cpeir-methodological-guidebook.html. [6]

UNECE (2019), *Third Environmental Performance Review of Kazakhstan*, United Nations Economic Commission for Europe, Geneva, https://www.unece.org/env/epr.html. [3]

US Department of Commerce (2018), *Kazakhstan Country Commercial Guide - Oil and Gas*, https://www.export.gov/article?id=Kazakhstan-Oil-and-Gas (accessed on 29 April 2019). [1]

World Bank (2019), "World Development Indicators GDP Growth (annual %)", (database), https://data.worldbank.org/indicator/NY.GDP.MKTP.KD.ZG (accessed on 18 January 2019). [2]

Notes

[1] Codes in Kazakhstan have a higher legal value than laws, which brings an indisputable value to this codification effort.

[2] See "Defining green finance" section of Chapter 2 for further details of what green finance may mean in Kazakhstan

2 Statistics on environmental expenditures in Kazakhstan: Current state of affairs

This chapter outlines work by Kazakhstan's Committee on Statistics with regard to implementation of the System of Environmental-Economic Account. It examines what kind of green finance is measured in the country, defining expenditures for environmental protection and resource management. It further offers a conceptual link between green finance and the country's statistical system on environmental and green economy expenditures. Through the use of available statistical data presented in 11 figures, this chapter also shows how much investment and current expenditures have been spent for environmental protection activities and examines where major data gaps exist.

What kind of green finance is measured in Kazakhstan?

The Committee on Statistics of the Ministry of National Economy (Committee on Statistics) has developed and manages the statistical database on current and investment expenditures for environmental protection, as well as the associated questionnaires used to collect data. The committee bases its environment-related statistical system on the Classification of Environmental Protection Activities (CEPA) under the System of Environmental-Economic Accounts (SEEA).[1] CEPA defines "environmental protection" as all purposeful activities and actions that directly aim to prevent, reduce and eliminate pollution or any other degradation of the environment resulting from production and consumption processes.

CEPA targets activities whose primary purpose is environmental protection. It thus excludes activities that aim principally to satisfy technical needs or internal health and safety requirements, or to mobilise and manage natural resources. It also excludes activities that aim primarily to produce and market environmental goods (since they do not directly aim at environmental protection, but rather at use of the goods produced). Savings of energy and raw materials are only included to the extent that they mainly aim at environmental protection.

This study uses the terms "current expenditure" and "investment expenditure" for environmental protection or resource management. These two terms are based on the instructions for the statistical forms for investment expenditures and costs of environmental protection. The study defines two different types of expenditures as follows:

- *Current expenditures*: expenses of entities to ensure ongoing work, technological processes and industries, as well as for the maintenance and operation of machinery and equipment, that are designed to prevent, reduce, clean or eliminate pollutants
- *Investment expenditures*: investment by entities in fixed assets, such as facilities, machinery, equipment and vehicles, to protect the environment or achieve rational use of natural resources (Committee on Statistics, 2017[1]), (Committee on Statistics, 2017[2]).

Figure 2.1 illustrates how relevant information on current and investment expenditures for environmental protection and resource management is collected. Statistical Form 161112108 collects data for investment. Statistical Form 151112212 collects data for environmental protection, including current (or operational) expenditures that are both provided by the Committee on Statistics.

Four types of expenses are collected through Statistical Form 151112212, of which this study uses the data collected as "current costs" as current expenditures for environmental protection. Apart from current costs, Kazakh entities report on their environmental payments, payments for resource use and compensation for damage (see the next sub-section for further details).

Figure 2.1 also shows which activities are measured as environmental protection and resource management activities in Kazakhstan's statistical system (at the bottom of the figure). Information related to investment expenditure captures all the categories on environmental protection (in accordance with CEPA), and renewable energy and energy efficiency, as well as other climate change mitigation activities. Conversely, current expenditures only capture environmental protection activities under CEPA.

Figure 2.1. Conceptual link between measurement of green finance and Kazakhstan's current statistical system on environmental and green economy expenditures

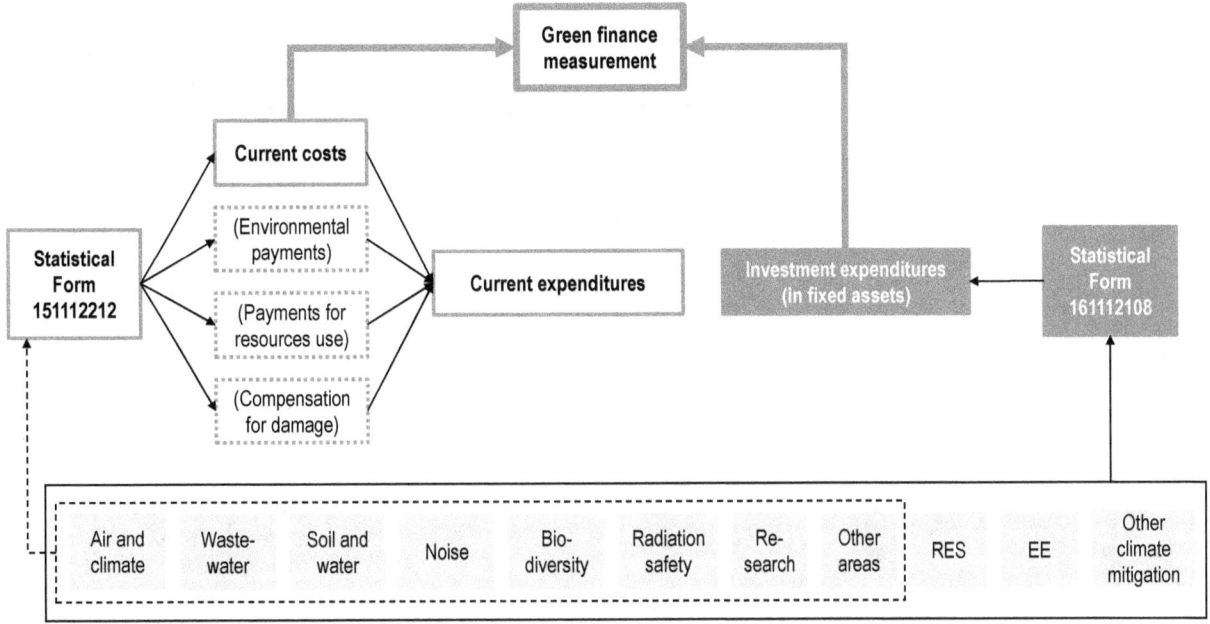

Note: RES: renewable energy sources. EE: energy efficiency. "Other climate mitigation" includes, but is not limited to, activities such as avoidance of fugitive gases.
Sources: Adapted from (Committee on Statistics, 2017[2]), https://stat.gov.kz/respondent/form; (Committee on Statistics, 2017[1]), https://stat.gov.kz/respondent/form.

The detailed instructions prepared by the Committee on Statistics provide definitions of certain environmental protection activities for which public- and private-sector entities are required to report their expenditures (Committee on Statistics, 2017[1]), (Committee on Statistics, 2017[2]). In addition, the instruction on investment expenditures also includes guidance about reporting investment in energy saving, renewable energy or other GHG reduction measures (See Table 2.1).

Table 2.1. Summary of definitions of expenditures for environmental protection and resource management

	Investment expenditures	Current expenditure
Environmental protection	<ul><li>protection of the environment and rational use of natural resources</li><li>commissioning and reconstruction of wastewater treatment plants</li><li>commissioning of facilities for cleaning household and drains</li><li>improvement of surface water quality protection of land resources</li><li>creation of specially protected nature areas.</li></ul>	<ul><li>maintenance and operation of fixed assets for environmental protection (without the cost of their modernisation and reconstruction): raw materials, fuel and electricity, personnel costs; insurance payments related to environmental facilities and equipment, etc.</li><li>costs of collection, storage/disposal and processing/neutralisation, destruction, disposal of production and consumption wastes on their own</li><li>control over the harmful effects on the environment, and monitoring activities, scientific and technical research, environmental management</li><li>operational measures for the preservation and restoration of the quality of the environment disturbed as a result of previously conducted economic activities</li><li>other measures to reduce the harmful effects on the environment.</li></ul>
Energy saving, renewable energy and other GHG reduction measures	<ul><li>investment in energy-saving technologies</li><li>cost of implementing legal, organisational, scientific, industrial, technical and economic measures aimed at efficient use of fuels and energy</li><li>investment in renewable energy</li><li>GHG emissions reduction or increase in GHG absorption, such as using flaring gas, reducing waste generation, ncreasing reuse/alternative use, using gas cleaning systems, eliminating sources of GHG emissions</li><li>investment in technology of producing goods and services for minimising environmental impact, preserving ecosystems, reducing use of resources, etc.</li></ul>	Not tracked as of 2019

Sources: Adapted from (Committee on Statistics, 2017[2]), https://stat.gov.kz/respondent/form; (Committee on Statistics, 2017[1]), https://stat.gov.kz/respondent/form.

This detailed guidance greatly helps clarify what activities and expenses each entity shall report as expenditures for environmental protection or certain resource management activities. The committee's instructions are particularly detailed and useful for categories of expenses (e.g. the definition of "maintenance costs" or "investment costs in investment"). However, they are less detailed about specific activities (e.g. what kind of activities should be considered as "protection of atmospheric air and problems of climate change").

Green finance that can contribute to implementation of the Green Economy Concept appears broader than the activities captured in the statistical forms and accompanying instructions. It is not enough to measure finance only for activities that aim primarily to protect the environment. For instance, the Statistical Forms do not clearly reflect measures for reduction of water resource consumption, rational use of forestry resources or climate change adaptation.

Further, the instructions do not detail key principles or performance criteria. When judging whether an activity should be reported as green finance, reporting entities have no reference point. Some activities are relatively easy to identify as green finance (e.g. solar panel and air pollution abatement). Others are less clear (e.g. energy efficiency for power plants, natural gas vehicles, climate change adaptation). Clearer principles or performance criteria for the latter would therefore be useful to better understand green finance flows in Kazakhstan and improve methodologies to measure such finance flows.

As discussed in Chapter 3, Kazakhstan's effort for clearer definitions of green finance could benefit from several international and national initiatives that aim to define and classify green or sustainable finance. For instance, the European Commission through its Technical Expert Group (TEG) has started to develop "a common sustainable finance taxonomy to ensure market consistency and clarity, starting with climate change" (HLEG, 2018[3]). An activity must satisfy one of the following four conditions to qualify as sustainable finance (TEG, 2018[4]):

- Contribute substantially to at least one of the six environmental objectives (i.e. climate change mitigation; climate change adaptation; sustainable use and protection of water and marine resources; transition to a circular economy, waste prevention and recycling; pollution prevention and control; and protection of healthy ecosystems).
- Do no significant harm to any of the other environmental objectives.
- Comply with minimum social safeguards.
- Comply with technical screening criteria.

How does Kazakhstan's national statistical system collect data?

The Committee on Statistics collects data on environmental expenditures in Kazakhstan, in accordance with CEPA and the Classification of Economic Activities of the Republic of Kazakhstan. The latter is equivalent to the International Standard Industrial Classification up to four digits (OECD, 2019[5]).

The committee collects information on investment expenditures (in fixed assets) and current (or operational) expenditures through two separate statistical forms (161112108 and 151112212). While the form on investment is used for reporting on various investment activities including on environment and resource management, the form on current environmental expenditures is specifically on environmental protection activities.

The statistical form on environmental protection (151112212) collects data on environmental expenditures. This form reports not only current (or operational) costs for environmental expenditures, but also four other types of expenses by entities as shown below:

1. **Current costs for environmental protection** are used as current expenditures for environmental protection in this study. This type includes expenses of public and private entities to ensure ongoing technological processes and industries, as well as to maintain and operate machinery and equipment used to prevent, reduce, clean, recycle or eliminate pollutants;
2. **Environmental payments** are expenses actually paid according to legislation for discharges, emissions of pollutants and waste, among others;
3. **Payments for the use of natural resources** mainly include payments for the use of surface water resources, land, wildlife, forests and protected natural areas;
4. **Compensation for damages** are fines and penalties collected by authorised state bodies for claims for damages due to violation of environmental legislation (Committee on Statistics, 2017[2]).

Current (or operational) expenditures in this report include only "current costs" among these four types. Current costs for environmental protection (type 1) account for 60% of total amount of the four types of expenses by the reporting entities. These costs have increased, in nominal terms, by about 60% from 2012 to 2017, amounting to KZT 175 billion (or USD 462 million[2]) in 2017 (see Figure 2.2). Reporting entities would also pay environmental payments, payments for resources use and compensations to the government authorities. However, such payments and compensations were not necessarily used directly for investment in, or operation of, environmental protection or resource management activities.

Figure 2.2. Trends in environmental expenses provided by Kazakh entities for environmental protection (excluding investment expenditures)

KZT billion - Nominal

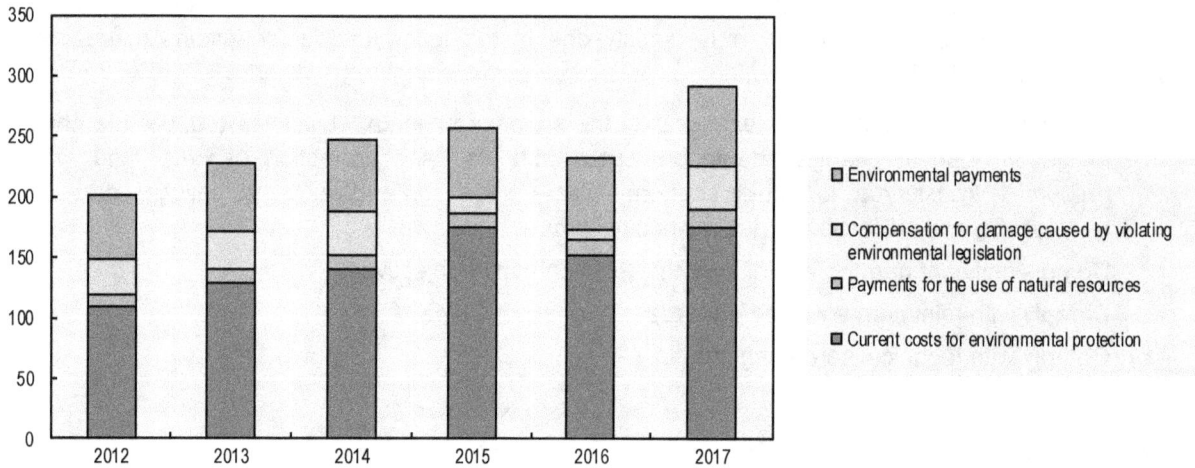

Sources: Adapted from (Committee on Statistics, 2017[2]), https://stat.gov.kz/respondent/form; (Committee on Statistics, 2017[1]), https://stat.gov.kz/respondent/form.

Green finance can be provided or channelled through several different financial sources, intermediaries and project developers. These channels generally have different implications for data availability and the ease of measuring financial flows. In Kazakhstan, they include republican (or national) and local governments, development partners, state-owned enterprises, private-sector entities and households. Kazakhstan's statistical system requires domestic public entities and all firms in the country's business registry to report on their investment and current expenditures for environmental protection, and on their investment in resource management (e.g. energy efficiency and renewable energy development) (OECD, 2019[5]).

Table 2.2 outlines different sources and state of tracking for the green economy transition. It highlights financial instruments; sources, intermediaries and project developers for investments; and which of these channels report on expenditure-related data to the Committee on Statistics. The statistical system does not require entities to report on which financial instruments were used for their environmental expenditures. This study therefore does not disaggregate the data on green finance flows by financial instrument. Such an approach could be an area for future analytical work on Kazakhstan's statistical system.

Table 2.2. Different sources and state of tracking

Sector	Sources/intermediaries/project developers	Examples of financial instruments	Reporting to the Committee on Statistics
Public	Domestic public finance (republican and local budgets)	Investment by republican and local budgets, and subsidies, including grants, for green activities	Yes
	Development financial institutions and bilateral donors (international)	Grants, concessional and non-concessional loans, bonds, equity and guarantees	No
Private	State-owned entities (e.g. Development Bank of Kazakhstan, Damu Fund, Samruk Kazyna, etc.)	Grants, concessional and non-concessional loans, bonds and equity	Yes (as private-sector entities)
	Private-sector entities based in Kazakhstan	Debt/equity financing Balance-sheet financing	Yes (those included in the business registry)
	Private-sector entities based outside Kazakhstan	Debt/equity financing Balance-sheet financing	No
	Households	Own revenues and expenses Debt financing	No

Sources: Adapted from (Committee on Statistics, 2017[2]), https://stat.gov.kz/respondent/form; (Committee on Statistics, 2017[1]), https://stat.gov.kz/respondent/form; (OECD, 2019[5]).

What figures do the available data sets show?

This sub-section uses available data to estimate the scale of current and investment expenditures for environmental protection activities, and to some extent, for resource management activities in Kazakhstan. Examples of resource management include renewable energy, energy efficiency and other climate mitigation actions such as avoidance of fugitive gases. It draws on data on the website of the Committee on Statistics, as well as on information from the pilot estimate under joint work by the OECD and the government of Kazakhstan on the SEEA. It first provides an overview of both current and investment expenditures, followed by separate and more detailed examination of each of them.

Overview: Current and investment expenditures

Table 2.3 shows the data on investment and current expenditures (current costs only)[3] for environmental protection. For both investment and current expenditures, the largest amounts were spent on air pollution, wastewater treatment and waste management, as well as on protection and rehabilitation of soil, groundwater and surface water. The table also shows a sharp rise in investment expenditures for renewable energy and energy efficiency from 2015-17, which amounted to nearly KZT 30 billion (USD 79 million) in nominal terms. It also marks substantial fluctuations in the volumes during the same period.

Table 2.3. Investment and current expenditures of environmental protection and certain resource management activities from 2015 to 2017

KZT million, nominal

Activity	CEPA[2] class	Investment expenditure			Current expenditure (current costs only)		
		2015	2016	2017	2015	2016	2017
Protection of atmospheric air and problems of climate change	CEPA 1	24 936	18 128	22 764	50 613	41 624	48 912
Wastewater treatment	CEPA 2	15 186	10 128	5 966	46 221	44 166	47 842
Waste management	CEPA 3	14 131	8 464	6 210	51 883	42 105	50 153
Protection and rehabilitation of soil, groundwater and surface water	CEPA 4	10 449	4 278	8 826	10 998	16 182	13 578
Noise and vibration effects reduction	CEPA 5	-	4	-	31	36	39
Conservation of biodiversity and habitat	CEPA 6	688	461	420	903	880	635
Radiation safety	CEPA 7	192	90	81	1 120	1 110	1 135
Scientific research	CEPA 8	333	621	129	2 935	3 333	4 038
Other areas of environmental protection	CEPA 9	16 969	1 761	42 568	9 946	2 770	9 112
Total (Environmental protection)		82 883	43 937	86 962	**174 650**	**152 206**	**175 445**
Renewable energy sources	-	7 488	956	18 885	n.a.	n.a.	n.a.
Energy-saving technologies and energy efficiency	-	656	155	15 612	n.a.	n.a.	n.a.
Other measures to reduce GHG emissions[1]	-	1 115	218	n.a.	n.a.	n.a.	n.a.
Total (Resource management)		**9 258**	**1 329**	**34 497**	**n.a.**	**n.a.**	**n.a.**

Notes:
1. These other measures are gas flaring, reduction of waste generation and increasing reuse or alternative use to reduce waste landfill, eliminating sources of GHG emissions.
2. **CEPA**: Classification for Environmental Protection Activities, **GHG**: Greenhouse gas, **n.a.**: information not available.

Sources: Adapted from (Committee on Statistics, 2017[2]), https://stat.gov.kz/respondent/form; (Committee on Statistics, 2017[1]), https://stat.gov.kz/respondent/form.

The level of investment and current expenditures (current costs only) for environmental protection as a share of GDP remains relatively low, compared to those of EU countries (see Figure 2.3). Investment as a share of GDP is 0.2% on average over the period between 2015 and 2017 and that of current expenditure (only current costs) is 0.4% for the same period. This is substantially lower than the targeted investment needs identified by the Green Economy Concept (1.0% of GDP), while recognising the data may have missed certain types of expenditures. Environmental expenditure per GDP in EU-28 countries accounts for 2.0% on average over the same period (for data on the European Union, see (Eurostat, n.d.[6])).

Figure 2.3. Investment and current expenditure for environmental protection as share of GDP

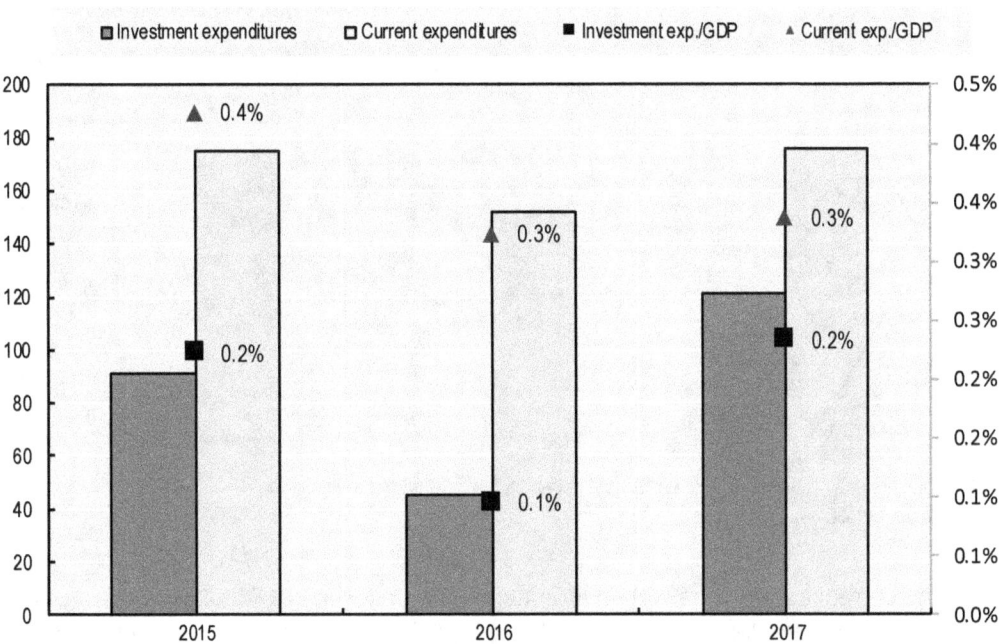

Note: Left axis: KZT; Right axis: percentage of GRP
Sources: Adapted from (Committee on Statistics, 2017[2]), https://stat.gov.kz/respondent/form; (Committee on Statistics, 2017[1]), https://stat.gov.kz/respondent/form; (World Bank, 2019[7]), https://data.worldbank.org/indicator/NY.GDP.MKTP.KD.ZG.

Current expenditures

Figure 2.4 illustrates how data on current environmental expenditures are disaggregated and at what levels these data are available. Disaggregated data on current expenditure (current costs in the figure) for environmental protection into private- and public-sector entities (and households) would be useful for the Kazakh government to analyse green finance flows within the country. However, the Committee on Statistics does not publish such data. Disaggregated data are available by region (i.e. 14 regions, as well as Astana City and Almaty City), as well as by activity for the data sets from the pilot estimate during 2015-17.

Figure 2.4. Availability of disaggregated data on current expenditure of environmental protection

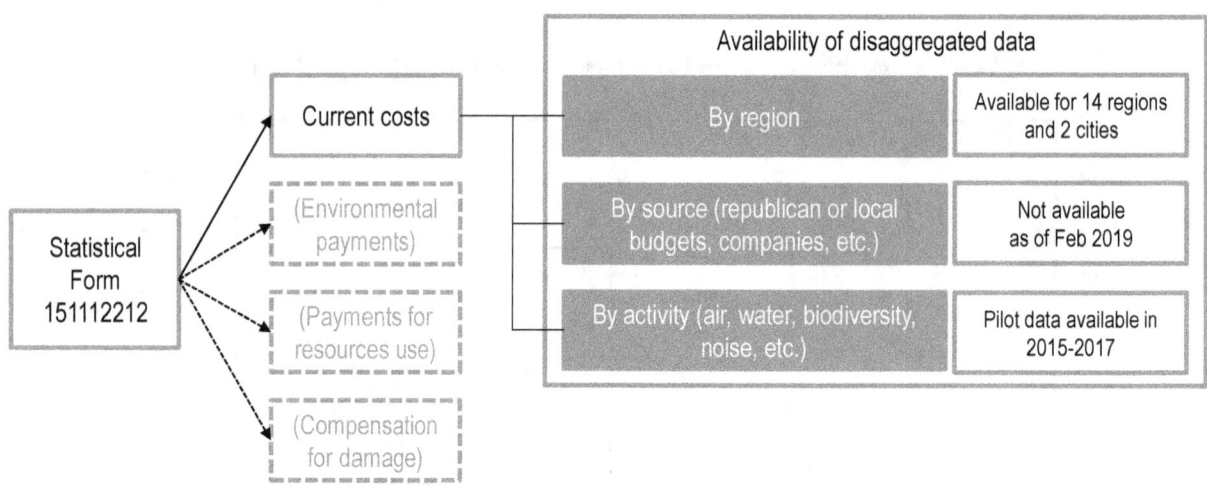

Note: This study considers only "current costs" to be "current expenditures" as part of green finance.
Source: Author's own elaborations

About 85% of the current expenditures for environmental protection in 2017 has been directed to protection of atmospheric air and problems of climate change (28%), wastewater treatment (27%) and waste management (29%). Current expenditures are also an important source for scientific research related to environmental protection, which accounts for 2%.

Current expenditures for environmental protection also vary substantially among oblasts (see Figure 2.5). For instance, Aktobe, Atyrau, Karaganda, Mangistau and Pavlodar oblasts record relatively large amounts of expenditure for environmental protection. This is partly due to the relatively large size of the economies and their structures. In terms of economic structure, Atyrau and Mangistau oblasts have relatively large shares of industrial, mining and extractive sectors in their gross regional product (GRP). Karaganda and Pavlodar oblasts have relatively large shares of manufacturing and energy sectors in their GRP. Aktobe has a relatively large share of mining and energy sectors in its GRP. Aktobe, Mangistau and Pavlodar also record relatively high shares of environmental expenditures per GRP compared to other regions (0.86%, 0.75% and 0.96% respectively).

Figure 2.5. Current environmental expenditures (current costs only) by region

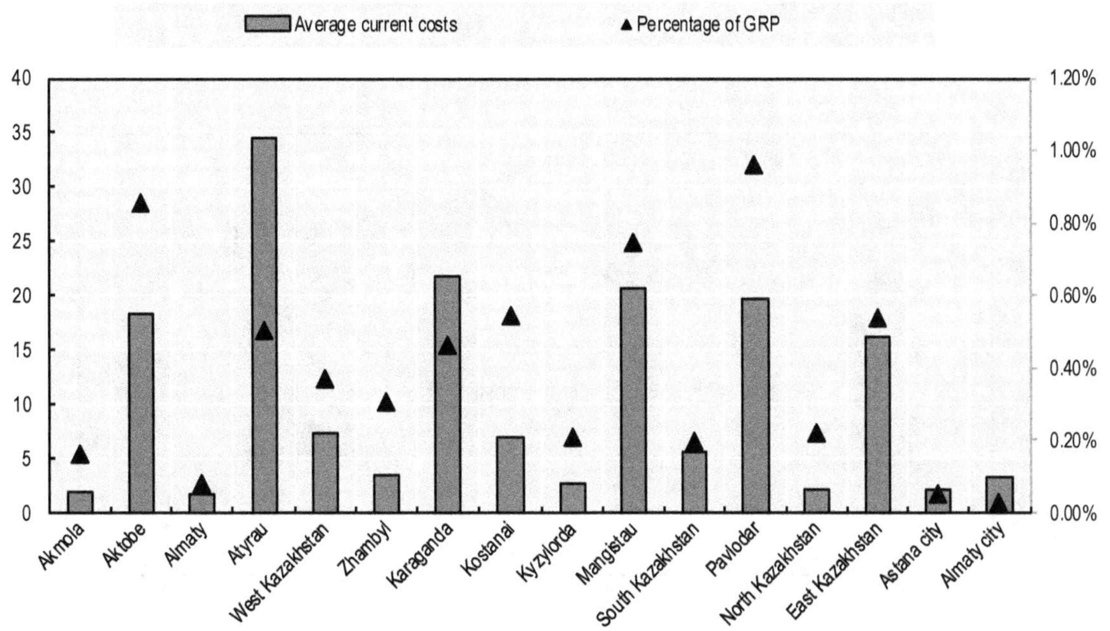

Note: Left axis: KZT billion annual average between 2015 and 2017; Right axis: percentage of GRP
Sources: Adapted from (Committee on Statistics, 2017[2]), https://stat.gov.kz/respondent/form; (Committee on Statistics, 2017[1]), https://stat.gov.kz/respondent/form.

Expenditures are expressed in nominal terms and the average annual inflation rate between 2012 and 2017 was about 7.8%. Hence, the increase is slightly smaller as shown in Figure 2.6. Discussion under the joint project on SEEA by the Committee on Statistics and the OECD also suggested that Kazakhstan explore and determine the most appropriate price index to derive the expenditure data in real terms (OECD, 2019[5]).

Figure 2.6. Trends in current expenditure for environmental protection (current costs only)

KZT – Nominal and real price in 2012

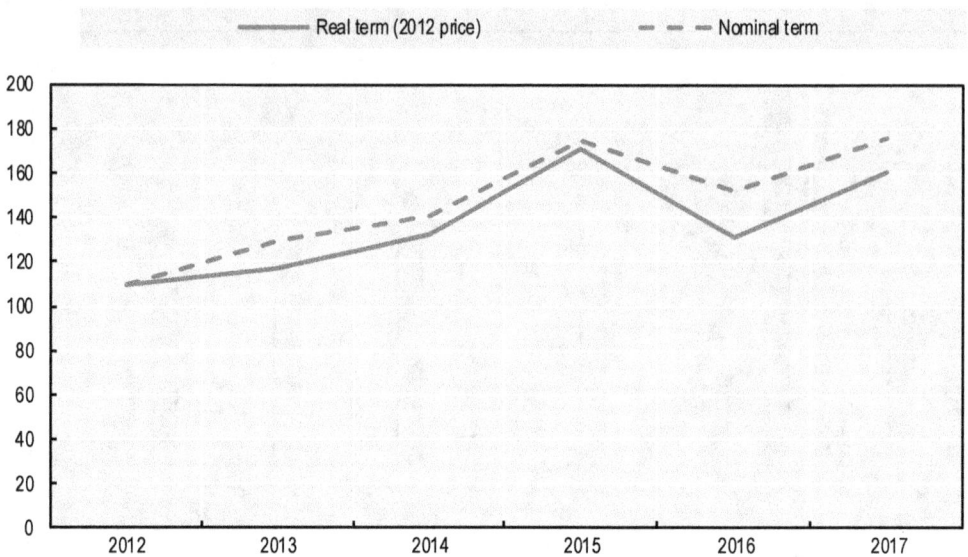

Sources: Adapted from (Committee on Statistics, 2017[2]), https://stat.gov.kz/respondent/form; (Committee on Statistics, 2017[1]), https://stat.gov.kz/respondent/form. GDP deflators are obtained from (World Bank, 2019[8]), https://data.worldbank.org/indicator/NY.GDP.DEFL.KD.ZG?end=2017&locations=KZ&start=2011&view=chart.

Different industrial sectors have different spending patterns for environmental protection. Figure 2.7 shows data on current environmental expenditures by the six economic sectors that spent the largest amounts for a three-year average over 2015-17. The mining and quarrying industry spent the largest volume of current expenditures for environmental protection activities, especially waste management (KZT 25 billion) and air pollution (KZT 13 billion). This seems natural given the nature of this industry. The manufacturing industry also spends a large amount of current environmental expenditures related to air pollution (KZT 26 billion), wastewater management (KZT 20 billion) and waste management (KZT 12 billion).

Figure 2.7. Top six industries spending current expenditures for environmental protection

KZT billion per year – average between 2015 and 2017

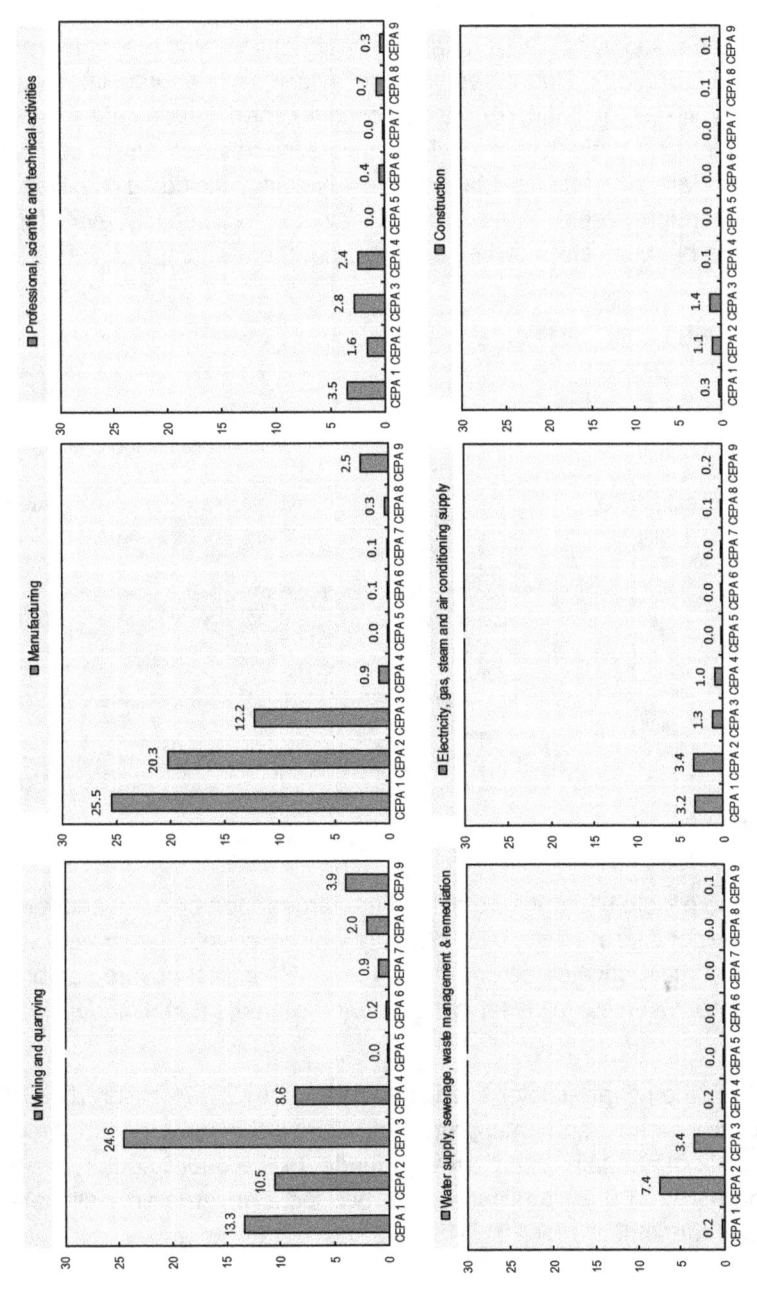

Notes:
1. **CEPA1**: Protection of ambient air and climate; **CEPA2**: Wastewater management; **CEPA3**: Waste management; **CEPA4**: Protection and remediation of soil, groundwater and surface water; **CEPA5**: Noise and vibration abatement (excluding workplace protection); **CEPA6**: Protection of biodiversity and landscapes; **CEPA7**: Protection against radiation (excluding external safety); **CEPA8**: Research and development; **CEPA9**: Other environmental protection activities.
2. For full data, see Annex 1.

Sources: Adapted from (Committee on Statistics, 2017[2]), https://stat.gov.kz/respondent/form; (Committee on Statistics, 2017[1]), https://stat.gov.kz/respondent/form.

Investment expenditures

Similar to current expenditures, the Committee on Statistics also collects data on investment expenditures from public and private-sector entities in accordance with CEPA, but through Statistical Form 161112108. In this way, the committee collects and maintains data on expenditures for fixed capital formation in various environmental protection activities along with other types of investment-related data in general.

Disaggregated data on investment expenditure of environmental protection are available by region, source and activity. This means the disaggregation of data for investment expenditure is more granular than that of current expenditures (Figure 2.8). Public-sector finance is disaggregated into republican and local budgets. For its part, private-sector finance consists of investment funded by individual entities' own sources and borrowed funds (e.g. bank loans). The private sector here also comprises state-owned enterprises, such as JSC Baiterek National Management Holding, including the Development Bank of Kazakhstan and JSC Sovereign Wealth Fund Samruk Kazyna. Yet publicly available statistics do not distinguish investment data by these state-owned entities from the rest of the private-sector entities.

Figure 2.8. Availability of disaggregated data on investment expenditure of environmental protection

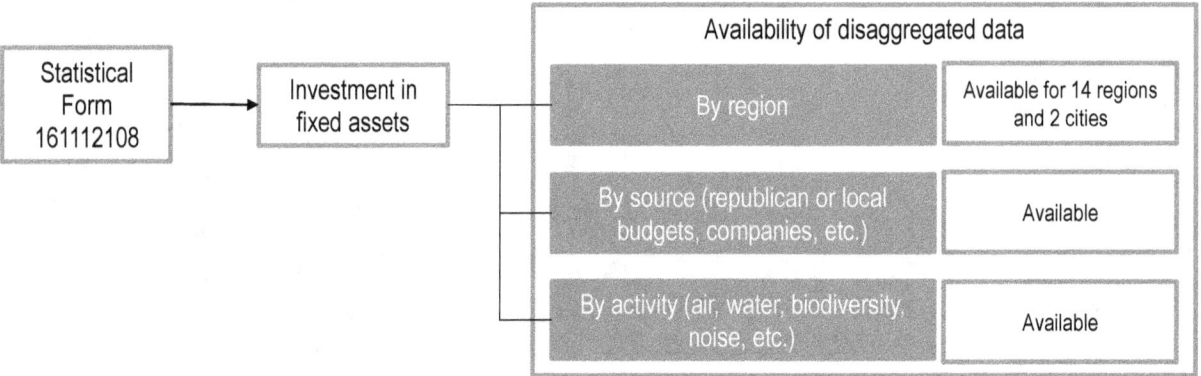

Source: Author's own elaborations

As shown in Figure 2.9, the private sector has provided the largest portion of investment in environmental protection (89% of total expenditure) over 2013-17. Data on the private investment markedly fluctuate. Further, the data show that most private-sector entities (i.e. 84% of total private sector finance) use their own funding, such as internal reserves, to invest in their environmental protection activities during the same period.

On average, over 2013-17, the private-sector entities spent about KZT 71 billion (USD 187.7 million) per year out of their own funding for environmental protection. During the same period, they spent about KZT 13.2 million (USD 34.9 million) annually with borrowed funds. In the public sector, the republican budget allocated KZT 4.5 billion (USD 11.9 million) per year, while local governments allocated KZT 5.4 billion (USD 14.2 million) on average annually for 2013-17.

Figure 2.9. Investment expenditures in environmental protection

KZT - Nominal

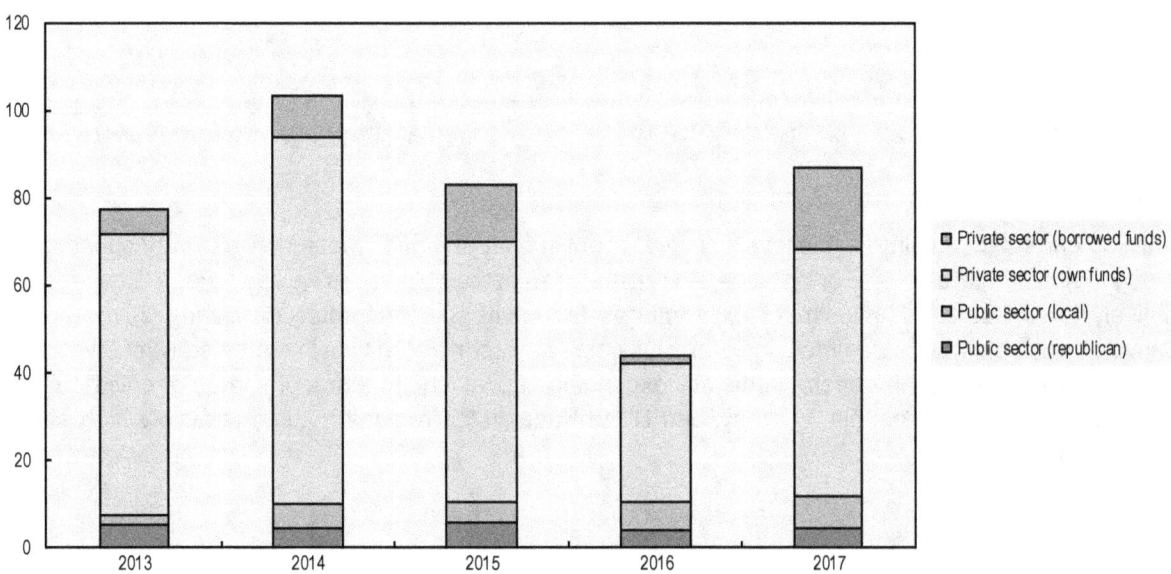

Sources: Adapted from (Committee on Statistics, 2017[2]), https://stat.gov.kz/respondent/form; (Committee on Statistics, 2017[1]), https://stat.gov.kz/respondent/form.

Of borrowed funds, the available statistics show that domestic bank lending was small (in 2013-14) or nearly non-existent (in 2015-17). It is not clear why bank loans financed such little investment, especially from 2015 to 2017. Nor is it clear why bank loans decreased from KZT 3.4 billion (USD 9 million) in 2013 to almost zero in recent years. As one potential reason, environmental protection activities cannot afford the high cost of capital (e.g. high interest rate). As a result, private-sector entities often tend not to take loans from banks. This rationale, however, does not explain the relatively high volume of bank loans in 2013. Identifying the underlying reasons may deserve further analytical work.

The data show notable variations in the amounts of investment in certain sectors such as wastewater management and "other areas". These could benefit from further examination (Table 2.4).

Apart from the salient number on the "other areas" category in 2017, investment in the "air pollution prevention and climate change" category shows the largest number of all (27.6% on average between 2013 and 2017). Meanwhile, climate change related activities here, by definition, do not include energy efficiency or renewable energy under CEPA. Another large part of investment has been spent on "wastewater treatment" (20.8% on average), followed by "protection and rehabilitation of soil, groundwater and surface water" (15.5%) and "waste management" (12.0%).

Table 2.4. Investment expenditures for environmental protection by activity

KZT million

	2012	2013	2014	2015	2016	2017
Protection of atmospheric air and problems of climate change	28 829	26 815	27 056	24 936	18 128	22 764
Wastewater treatment	20 119	18 775	41 812	15 186	10 128	5 966
Waste management	10 777	8 026	16 941	14 131	8 464	6 210
Protection and rehabilitation of soil, groundwater and surface water	7 597	10 612	13 436	10 449	4 278	8 826

	2012	2013	2014	2015	2016	2017
Reduction of noise and vibration effects	22	5	126	–	4	–
Conservation of biodiversity and habitat	379	135	164	688	461	420
Radiation safety	451	197	71	192	90	81
Scientific research	454	722	790	333	621	129
Other areas of environmental protection	6 522	12 213	3 096	16 969	1 761	42 568

Sources: Adapted from (Committee on Statistics, 2017[2]), https://stat.gov.kz/respondent/form; (Committee on Statistics, 2017[1]), https://stat.gov.kz/respondent/form.

Similar to current expenditures, the levels of investment in environmental protection also vary substantially among regions (Figure 2.10). For instance, Atyrau and Mangistau oblasts, as well as Astana City, recorded relatively large scales of investment expenditures for environmental protection during 2015-17. The relatively large volume of investment in Astana City may have correlated with the large scale of investment in fixed capital formation in general in the still expanding capital city. In terms of shares of environmental expenditures per GRP, Akmola, Zhambyl and North Kazakhstan regions marked relatively high shares over 2015-17.

Figure 2.10. Investment environmental expenditures by region

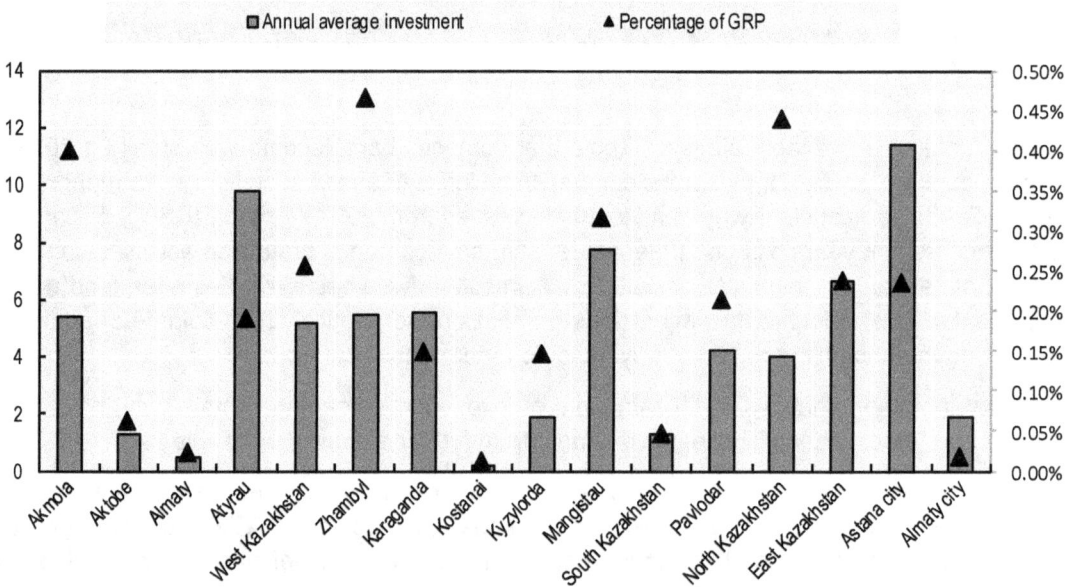

Note: Left axis: KZT billion annual average between 2015 and 2017; Right axis: percentage of GRP
Sources: Adapted from (Committee on Statistics, 2017[2]), https://stat.gov.kz/respondent/form; (Committee on Statistics, 2017[1]), https://stat.gov.kz/respondent/form.

Figure 2.11 shows data on investment environmental expenditures by six economic sectors that spent the largest amounts during 2015-17. The numbers shown are a three-year average over the period. Similar to current expenditures, the mining industry invested the largest amount in environmental protection activities. Within these activities, they invested especially in air pollution abatement (KZT 7.0 billion) and wastewater management (KZT 6.0 billion).

The energy sector (i.e. electricity, gas, heat and air conditioning supply) also provided a substantial amount of investment. This was especially true for "other environmental activities", although the types of activities included in this category are not clear. The energy sector also substantially invested in air pollution abatement (KZT 4.0 billion) and waste management (KZT 3.0 billion). Similarly, the public administration sector invested a large amount in environmental protection. Its activities included air pollution abatement, protection and remediation of soil, groundwater and surface water, as well as wastewater management. The manufacturing sector invested KZT 7.0 billion per year in air pollution abatement, which was the largest amount for one single class of activity.

Figure 2.11. Top six industries spending investment expenditures for environmental protection and their purposes by CEPA class

KZT billion per year – average between 2015 and 2017

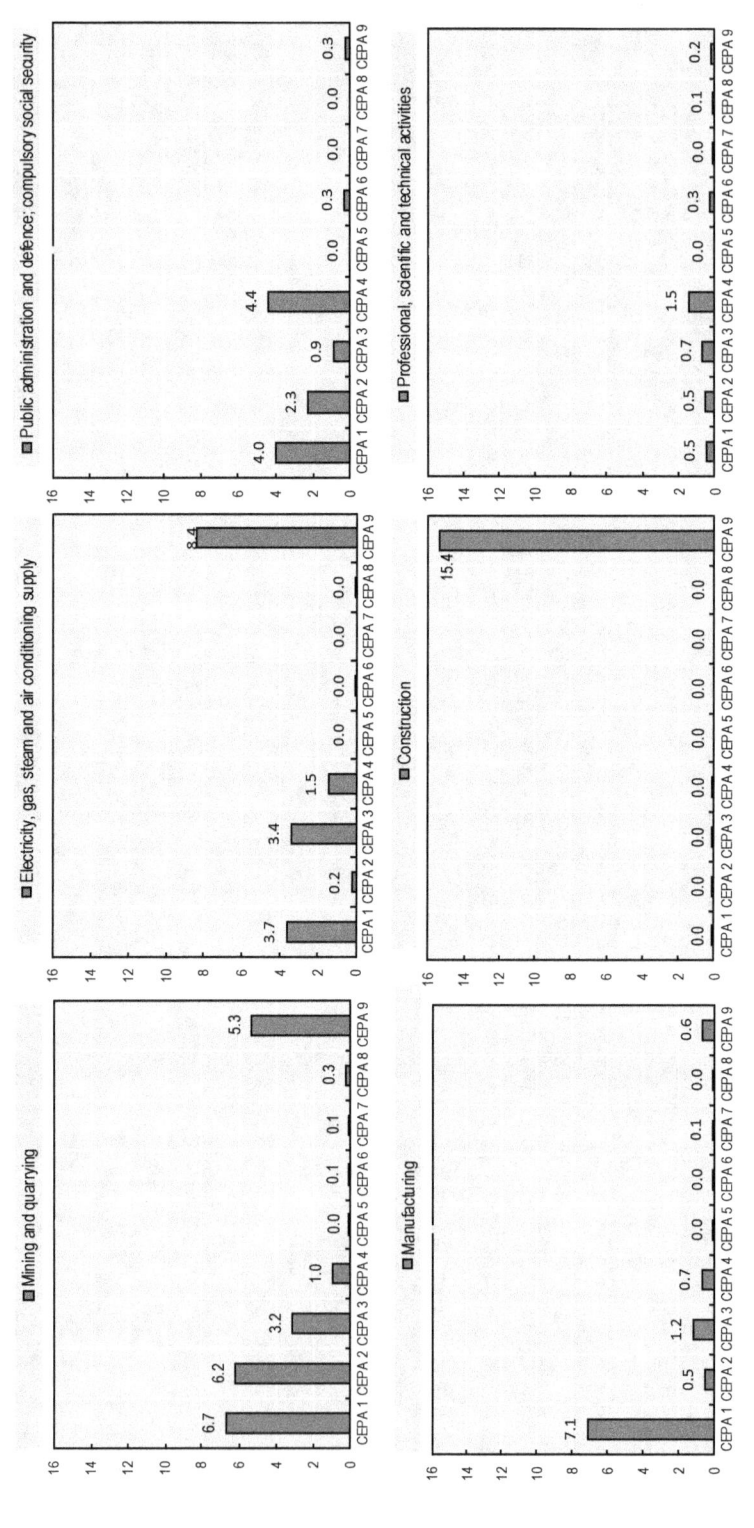

Notes:
1. **CEPA1**: Protection of ambient air and climate; **CEPA2**: Wastewater management; **CEPA3**: Waste management; **CEPA4**: Protection and remediation of soil, groundwater and surface water; **CEPA5**: Noise and vibration abatement (excluding workplace protection); **CEPA6**: Protection of biodiversity and landscapes; **CEPA7**: Protection against radiation (excluding external safety); **CEPA8**: Research and development; **CEPA9**: Other environmental protection activities.
2. For full data, see Annex 1.

Sources: Adapted from (Committee on Statistics, 2017[2]), https://stat.gov.kz/respondent/form; (Committee on Statistics, 2017[1]), https://stat.gov.kz/respondent/form.

The statistical form for investment also includes the following three categories as investment activities related to "green economy":

- investment in renewable energy sources
- investment in energy saving and efficiency
- investment aimed at GHG reduction.

The instruction by the Committee on Statistics shows the three categories include investment in gas flaring, reduction of waste generation and increasing reuse or alternative use to reduce waste landfill, and eliminating sources of GHG emissions. This is especially the case for "investment aimed at GHG reduction" (Committee on Statistics, 2017[1]).

As Table 2.5 shows, the amounts of investment in those activities captured through the statistical form vary markedly, with a substantial hike in 2017. This study could not identify the underlying causes of such a significant change. However, it is relatively common that data on investment expenditures tend to fluctuate to a greater extent than data on current expenditures.

Table 2.5. Investment expenditure for "green economy" related activities

KZT million

	2012	2013	2014	2015	2016	2017
Investments in renewable energy sources	–	9 042	490	7 488	956	18 885
Investments in energy-saving technologies and energy efficiency	–	906	872	656	155	15 612
Investments aimed at reducing greenhouse gas emissions	–	–	413	1 115	218	–

Sources: Adapted from (Committee on Statistics, 2017[2]), https://stat.gov.kz/respondent/form; (Committee on Statistics, 2017[1]), https://stat.gov.kz/respondent/form.

Annex 2.A. Full data on current and investment expenditures for environmental protection by sector and by CEPA class

Annex Table 2.A.1. Current expenditures for environmental protection by sector and by CEPA class

KZT million: three-year average between 2015 and 2017

	CEPA 1	CEPA 2	CEPA 3	CEPA 4	CEPA 5	CEPA 6	CEPA 7	CEPA 8	CEPA 9	Total (2015-17 average)
Agriculture, forestry and fishing	53	37	161	37	1	0	0	4	10	303
Industry	42 262	41 604	41 456	10 628	27	313	1 088	2 469	6 710	146 557
Mining and quarrying	13 333	10 519	24 567	8 598	14	195	940	2 024	3 912	64 102
Manufacturing	25 494	20 250	12 230	862	10	114	140	304	2 492	61 896
Electricity, gas, steam and air conditioning supply	3 194	3 388	1 256	994	3	4	6	107	237	9 189
Water supply, sewerage, waste management and remediation	240	7 446	3 403	174	0	1	3	34	68	11 369
Construction	294	1 074	1 375	143	0	3	1	134	72	3 095
Wholesale and retail trade; repair of motor vehicles and motorcycles	152	172	290	17	0	0	1	6	45	683
Transportation and storage	562	597	700	318	6	73	24	138	154	2 572
Accommodation and food service activities	4	90	118	3	0	0	0	0	2	220
Information and communication	6	12	50	0	0	0	0	0	1	70
Financial and insurance activities	7	18	32	0	0	0	0	0	0	59
Real estate activities	50	153	226	6	0	0	0	0	5	440
Professional, scientific and technical activities	3 461	1 647	2 814	2 431	1	417	7	681	261	11 719
Administrative and support service activities	9	39	165	3	0	0	0	4	6	226
Public administration and defence; compulsory social security	102	151	172	0	0	0	0	0	4	431
Education	21	264	135	0	1	0	0	0	2	422
Human health and social work activities	43	179	312	1	0	0	0	0	0	535
Arts, entertainment and recreation	16	12	16	2	0	0	0	0	1	42
Other services	7	26	24	0	0	0	0	0	2	58
Total	47 050	46 076	48 047	13 586	35	806	1 122	3 436	7 276	167 434

Note: **CEPA1**: Protection of ambient air and climate; **CEPA2**: Wastewater management; **CEPA3**: Waste management; **CEPA4**: Protection and remediation of soil, groundwater and surface water; **CEPA5**: Noise and vibration abatement (excluding workplace protection); **CEPA6**: Protection of biodiversity and landscapes; **CEPA7**: Protection against radiation (excluding external safety); **CEPA8**: Research and development; **CEPA9**: Other environmental protection activities.
Sources: Adapted from (Committee on Statistics, 2017[2]), https://stat.gov.kz/respondent/form; (Committee on Statistics, 2017[1]), https://stat.gov.kz/respondent/form.

Annex Table 2.A.2. Investment expenditures for environmental protection by sector and by CEPA class

KZT million: three-year average between 2015 and 2017

	CEPA 1	CEPA 2	CEPA 3	CEPA 4	CEPA 5	CEPA 6	CEPA 7	CEPA 8	CEPA 9	Total (2015-17 average)
Agriculture, forestry and fishing	0	22	1	0	0	0	0	0	109	87
Industry	17 485	7 649	7 786	3 219	2	64	115	289	14 395	51 004
Mining and quarrying	6 708	6 189	3 170	985	0	63	55	276	5 332	22 778
Manufacturing	7 123	493	1 162	689	1	2	61	7	620	10 154
Electricity, gas, steam and air conditioning supply	3 654	207	3 435	1 455	0	1	0	12	8 429	17 188
Water supply, sewerage, waste management and remediation	0	760	19	90	0	0	0	0	22	884
Construction	1	0	0	8	0	0	0	0	15 401	7 711
Wholesale and retail trade; repair of motor vehicles and motorcycles	0	0	1	0	0	0	0	0	0	1
Transportation and storage	18	1	1	0	0	0	1	0	0	21
Accommodation and food service activities	0	0	0	0	0	0	0	0	0	0
Information and communication	16	0	0	0	0	0	0	0	0	16
Financial and insurance activities	0	0	6	0	0	0	0	0	0	6
Real estate activities	0	7	2	0	0	0	0	0	0	6
Professional, scientific and technical activities	463	489	653	1 457	0	261	5	72	175	3 574
Administrative and support service activities	0	0	0	0	0	0	0	0	0	1
Public administration and defence; compulsory social security	3 959	2 268	888	4 357	0	297	0	0	269	10 751
Education	0	0	0	0	0	0	0	0	0	0
Human health and social work activities	1	0	0	0	0	0	0	0	0	1
Arts, entertainment and recreation	0	0	0	0	0	0	0	0	0	0
Other services	0	0	800	0	0	0	0	0	581	981
Total	21 943	10 427	9 601	7 851	2	523	121	361	20 433	71 261

Note: **CEPA1**: Protection of ambient air and climate; **CEPA2**: Wastewater management; **CEPA3**: Waste management; **CEPA4**: Protection and remediation of soil, groundwater and surface water; **CEPA5**: Noise and vibration abatement (excluding workplace protection); **CEPA6**: Protection of biodiversity and landscapes; **CEPA7**: Protection against radiation (excluding external safety); **CEPA8:** Research and development; **CEPA9**: Other environmental protection activities.
Sources: Adapted from (Committee on Statistics, 2017[2]), https://stat.gov.kz/respondent/form; (Committee on Statistics, 2017[1]), https://stat.gov.kz/respondent/form.

Annex 2.B. Work by the Committee on Statistics

The Committee on Statistics has developed and manages the statistical database on current and investment expenditures for environmental protection, as well as the associated questionnaires used to collect data. The committee publishes information on current and investment expenditures through the following two annual reports:

1. **Report on environmental protection expenditures**[4]: this provides data on, among others, current expenditures for environmental protection, environmentally related payments and payments for natural resources;
2. **Report on investment activity**[5]: this provides data on investments in fixed assets, including, but not limited to, those in activities for environmental protection and green economy transition such as renewable energy, energy efficiency and other types of climate change mitigation.

The Committee on Statistics produces environmental-economic accounts based on environmental statistics and administrative data. These come from sources such as the Ministry of Agriculture, the Ministry of Energy, the Ministry of Finance, and the Ministry for Investments and Development. The Committee on Statistics has been working to align the country's statistical system with the System of Environmental-Economic Accounting 2012 – Central Framework (SEEA 2012 Central Framework).[6] Through the collaboration with the OECD, the committee conducted pilot calculations (based on available data) that covered the following SEEA accounts and years:

- physical flow account for energy for 2014-17
- air emission account for air pollutants for 2014-17
- solid waste account for 2016-17
- environmental protection expenditure account for 2015-17
- environmental tax account for 2013-17
- asset account for mineral and energy resources (for 19 main mineral and energy resources) for 2014-17.

Among these accounts, the environmental protection expenditure accounts (EPEA) is particularly relevant to this study on measuring green finance flows. EPEA also relates to a number of other accounts in the SEEA, particularly the Environmental Goods and Services Sector. The Committee on Statistics compiled the pilot EPEA based on SEEA and the Eurostat Handbook on Environmental Protection Expenditure Accounts.

> **Annex Box 2.B.1. Environmentally beneficial subsidies in Kazakhstan**
>
> Kazakhstan has both environmentally preferable and harmful subsidy schemes. On the preferable subsidies, the law of the Republic of Kazakhstan "On support for the use of renewable energy sources" specifies the country provides individual consumers with targeted assistance for half the cost of installations for the use of renewable energy sources with a total power of no more than 5 kW. The tariff for 1 kWh of electricity generated is set at different levels: KZT 22.68 for wind power, KZT 34.61 for solar power, KZT 16.71 for small hydropower and KZT 32.23 for biogas (as of March 2019). It remains unclear how such public expenses for the subsidies have been captured in Kazakhstan's national statistical system, which hence may deserve further examination.
>
> Source: (Government of Kazakhstan, 2009[9]), http://adilet.zan.kz/rus/docs/Z090000165.

There is a range of databases outside Kazakhstan's national statistical system, which could help the country measure green finance flows. International public databases include AIDDATA, OECD DAC-Credit Reporting System, Eastern Partnership Transport Projects Database, World Bank Private Participation in Infrastructure Database, and databases of development financial institutions. Commercial databases include Bloomberg New Energy Finance, Dealogic, IJGlobal and Thomson ONE. Domestic institutions include Kazakh Invest and the national development funds and banks.

References

Committee on Statistics (2017), *Instruction for completing the statistical form national statistical observation "Report on the costs of protection environment "*, Committee on Statistics under Ministry of National Economy, Nur-Sultan, https://stat.gov.kz/respondent/form. [2]

Committee on Statistics (2017), *Instructions for completing the statistical form of nationwide statistical observation "Report on investment activity"*, Appendix 4 to the order Chairman of the Committee on Statistics of the Ministry National Economy of the Republic of Kazakhstan, Nur-Sultan, https://stat.gov.kz/respondent/form. [1]

Eurostat (n.d.), *Environmental Protection Expenditure Accounts: National Expenditure on Environmental Protection 2006-2017*, https://ec.europa.eu/eurostat/statistics-explained/index.php?title=Environmental_protection_expenditure_accounts#General_overview. [6]

Government of Kazakhstan (2009), *Law of the Republic of Kazakhstan "On support for the use of renewable energy sources*, http://adilet.zan.kz/rus/docs/Z090000165_ (accessed on 12 February 2020). [9]

HLEG (2018), *Financing a Sustainable European Economy: Final Report 2018 by the High-Level Expert Group on Sustainable Finance - Secretariat provided by the European Commission*, High-Level Expert Group on Sustainable Finance, Brussels, https://ec.europa.eu/info/sites/info/files/180131-sustainable-finance-final-report_en.pdf. [3]

OECD (2019), *Agreement between the government of the Republic of Kazakhstan and the Organisation for Economic Co-operation and Development for the realisation of the project "Implementation of the System of Environmental Economic Accounting": Interim Report*, OECD, Paris. [5]

TEG (2018), *Taxonomy pack for feedback and workshops invitations December 2019*, Technical Expert Group on Sustainable Finance, Brussels, https://ec.europa.eu/info/sites/info/files/business_economy_euro/banking_and_finance/documents/sustainable-finance-taxonomy-feedback-and-workshops_en.pdf. [4]

World Bank (2019), *World Development Indicators GDP Growth (annual %)*, (database), https://data.worldbank.org/indicator/NY.GDP.MKTP.KD.ZG (accessed on 18 January 2019). [7]

World Bank (2019), *World Development Indicators: Inflation, GDP Deflator (annual %)*, (database), https://data.worldbank.org/indicator/NY.GDP.DEFL.KD.ZG?end=2017&locations=KZ&start=2011&view=chart (accessed on 4 April 2019). [8]

Notes

[1] For further information, see:
https://ec.europa.eu/eurostat/statistics-explained/index.php?title=Glossary:Classification_of_environmental_protection_activities_(CEPA)

[2] Using the exchange rate between US Dollar and Kazakh tenge by the National Bank of Kazakhstan (KZT 378.29 = USD 1 as of 4 April 2019).

[3] These current (operational) expenditures only include current costs which enterprises and organisations spent to conduct events, ensure ongoing work technological processes and industries, and maintain and operate machinery and equipment.

[4] For the latest reports, see:
http://stat.gov.kz/faces/wcnav_externalId/homeNumbersEnvironment?_afrLoop=840975243553685#%40%3F_afrLoop%3D840975243553685%26_adf.ctrl-state%3D1jwbs8noj_43

[5] For the latest reports, see:
http://stat.gov.kz/faces/wcnav_externalId/homeNumbersInvestment?_afrLoop=840973946095242#%40%3F_afrLoop%3D840973946095242%26_adf.ctrl-state%3D1jwbs8noj_30

[6] This work conducted with various partners, including the OECD under the project "Introduction of the System of Environmental-Economic Accounting" as part of the Kazakhstan country programme between the government of Kazakhstan and the OECD. The SEEA 2012 Central Framework was produced under the auspices of the United Nations Statistics Division, the Statistical Office of the European Union (Eurostat), the Food and Agriculture Organization of the United Nations, the OECD, the International Monetary Fund and the World Bank Group. It was endorsed as an international standard by the United Nations Statistical Commission in 2012.

3 Informing further development: International initiatives on measuring financial flows for green economy

This chapter provides a brief overview of selected international standards and guidelines on classifications and taxonomies. These are related to environmental protection, resource management and broader activities for sustainable development. It highlights the work of the Astana International Financial Centre on green finance taxonomy. It also notes work by the OECD on environmental protection expenditure and revenues, including by the Research Collaborative on Tracking Finance for Climate Action. It discusses how such standards and guidelines can inform improvement of the approaches to measuring green finance flows in Kazakhstan. By leveraging them, the country could further strengthen its statistical system and develop a methodology to track green finance regularly.

Context

The government of Kazakhstan lacks a common definition of green finance and insight into spending on different policy areas related to the green economy transition. More knowledge in both these areas could help the country better understand flows of green finance (OECD, 2016[1]). As previously discussed, a range of data is readily available on expenditures for environmental protection in the country. Yet it would still be useful to clarify definitions of green finance in Kazakhstan. Specifically, the government could examine how to expand thematic coverage and improve the granularity of data under its statistical system. To inform further development of its methodologies to measuring green finance flows, Kazakhstan would benefit from initiatives within and outside the country at both the international and the European Union (EU) levels.

A range of institutions and countries has launched or implemented initiatives that directly or indirectly measure finance flows for green economy or climate action at a country-level. For instance, the European Statistical Office (Eurostat) has been operating the following data collection under the System of Environmental-Economic Accounting (SEEA):

- Environmental Goods and Services Sector (EGSS), using the Classifications of Environmental Protection Activities (CEPA) and the Classification of Resource Management Activities (CReMA)
- Environmental Protection Expenditure Accounts (EPEA) using CEPA.

CReMA could provide a useful framework for understanding financial flows for a wider range of resource management activities than renewable energy, energy efficiency and other climate change mitigation. However, implementation of CReMA might also involve certain technical challenges in Kazakhstan as discussed later in the sub-section on CReMA.

Further, the combination of CEPA and CReMA would not necessarily ensure measurement of a complete set of data on green finance flows for all actions that contribute to the green economy transition. For instance, certain climate change adaptation activities do not fall into either classification. As one complementary approach, the government could develop a more comprehensive taxonomy of green or sustainable finance.

Varying understanding of what green finance means among different countries and institutions has also been an issue discussed in several international forums, including the Technical Expert Group (TEG) on Sustainable Finance of the European Commission. With support from TEG, the European Commission was developing the EU Taxonomy of Sustainable Economic Activities as of March 2019.

In Kazakhstan, the Astana International Financial Centre began developing the taxonomy of green finance for Kazakhstan in early 2019. A Kazakhstan-specific green finance taxonomy would be useful to complement government efforts to further refine or develop definitions of activities for the country's green economy transition. Indeed, the taxonomy is being developed in part to help measure and report the flows and environmental impact of green projects (Ma, 2019[2]).

The Organisation for Economic Co-operation and Development (OECD) with its member countries has also continuously improved the environment-related statistical system, including on Environmental Protection Expenditure and Revenues (EPER). Work under the OECD-hosted Research Collaborative on Tracking Finance for Climate Action could also provide Kazakhstan with insight into technical aspects of tracking investment in certain areas of climate action and identifying the underlying sources of finance.

Table 3.1 outlines different standards, classifications and initiatives to be discussed in this section. By leveraging them, Kazakhstan could further strengthen the country's statistical system and develop a methodology to track green finance regularly. The subsequent sub-sections provide more detailed information on each standard or classification, and their implications for developing methodologies to measure green finance flows.

Table 3.1. Selected standards and classifications and their possible contributions to improving methodologies to measure green finance in Kazakhstan

Standards and classifications	Implications for improvement of green finance measurement in Kazakhstan
Classification of Environmental Protection Activities (CEPA)	Improve quality of already reported classes of data through further convergence with CEPA under SEEA
Classification of Resource Management Activities (CReMA)	Complement CEPA to cover a broader picture of activities for green economy transition, especially on activities for better resource management such as resource efficiency
Draft EU Taxonomy of Sustainable Economic Activities and other national-level work on taxonomies	Broaden coverage of categories to be reported on, and refine criteria for activities to be eligible as green/sustainable finance
	Support development of a Kazakhstan-specific Green Finance Taxonomy by following discussion on the EU and other national-level taxonomies of sustainable finance or activities
OECD work on Environmental Protection Expenditure and Revenues	Improve quality of already reported classes of data under CEPA through further convergence under SEEA
Research Collaborative on Tracking Finance for Climate Action	Improve methodologies for measuring investment and financial flows for activities that contribute to or inhibit climate change action at a national level
Climate Public Expenditures and Institutional Review	Improve methodologies for measuring financial flows for climate change action

Sources: Adopted from (Eurostat, 2016[3]), https://ec.europa.eu/eurostat/documents/3859598/7700432/KS-GQ-16-008-EN-N.pdf/f4965221-2ef0-4926-b3de-28eb4a5faf47;
(OECD, 2014[4]), https://www.oecd.org/statistics/datacollection/Environmental%20Data_SOE%20guidelines.pdf;
(OECD, n.d.[5]), https://www.oecd.org/env/researchcollaborative/;
(TEG, 2018[6]), https://ec.europa.eu/info/sites/info/files/business_economy_euro/banking_and_finance/documents/sustainable-finance-taxonomy-feedback-and-workshops_en.pdf;
(UNDP, 2015[7]), http://www.asia-pacific.undp.org/content/rbap/en/home/library/democratic_governance/cpeir-methodological-guidebook.html;

Existing and upcoming initiatives that can inform regular measurement of green finance flows in Kazakhstan

Classification of Environmental Protection Activities (CEPA)

CEPA is recognised as the international standard for collecting environmentally related expenditures in both fixed capital formation (i.e. investment expenditures) and current (or operational) expenditures. It is a comprehensive framework to cover purposeful activities directly aimed at prevention, reduction and elimination of pollution or degradation of the environment. EPEA under SEEA uses CEPA to classify environmental protection activities.

Kazakhstan based its national statistical system for environmental protection activities, including on expenditures, on the version of CEPA adopted by the UN Statistical Commission in 2002 (CEPA 2000). Hence, it would make sense that any methodology to regularly track green finance in Kazakhstan would build on the existing Kazakh database that is largely in line with CEPA 2000. Classes under CEPA 2000 are listed below:

- protection of ambient air and climate (CEPA 1)
- wastewater management (CEPA 2)
- waste management (CEPA 3)
- protection and remediation of soil, groundwater and surface water (CEPA 4)
- noise and vibration abatement (excluding workplace protection) (CEPA 5)
- protection of biodiversity and landscapes (CEPA 6)
- protection against radiation (excluding external safety) (CEPA 7)
- research and development (CEPA 8)

- other environmental protection activities (CEPA 9).

Environmental protection expenditure is defined as the economic resources (i.e. all transactions in monetary terms) that resident units devote to environmental protection. Environmental protection expenditure accounts for all production costs through the recording of the value of the outputs produced and the value of the uses of these outputs. This includes calculated cost items such as depreciation (i.e. consumption of fixed capital) or the cost of capital. The expenditure concept excludes the following:

- payments of interest, fines and penalties for non-compliance with environmental regulations or compensations to third parties
- payments of environmentally related taxes, as these taxes do not directly aim at environmental protection
- expenditure by enterprises for producing market environmental goods, such as production costs for equipment, materials and other parts of the environmental goods and services industry (such expenditure is recorded in statistics and account on EGSS).

The outcomes of the joint project by the Committee on Statistics and the OECD on "implementation of the SEEA" can inform development of approaches to measuring green finance flows. The project concluded that data sources were of good quality (OECD, 2019[8]). At the same, it identified several areas where the government could improve alignment with CEPA. For instance, the data available does not distinguish between expenditures made by businesses, governments and households. The statistical system also does not break expenditures down into environmental protection-specific services, connected products, adapted goods[1] and capital formation (OECD, 2019[8]).

Classification of Resource Management Activities (CReMA)

Despite its relevance to measuring green finance flows in Kazakhstan, CEPA does not capture some important activities for the country's transition to a green economy. Among others, these exclusions are energy saving with the aim of resource efficiency, production of energy by renewable sources and more efficient use of water, forest or mineral resources. CReMA could complement such a methodological gap by collecting information on relevant current and investment expenditures.

As part of SEEA 2012 Central Framework, Eurostat aims to complement CEPA with CReMA to capture resource management activities in national statistics. It is not mandatory in Europe to collect expenditure-related information on resource management activities. As of March 2019, however, there has been an interest in a pilot estimate of such expenditures using CReMA (Eurostat, 2018[9]). The European Statistical System Committee endorsed the European Strategy for Environmental Accounts 2019-23 in February 2019. The strategy includes Resource Management Expenditure Accounts as a priority area for development. This is especially the case in the field of expenditure related to renewable energy resources, energy savings and material recovery (European Statistical System Committee, 2019[10]). It recognises the Resource Management Expenditure Accounts as a necessary part of SEEA to complete the picture of environmental activities alongside EPEA, EGSS, and taxes and subsidies (European Statistical System Committee, 2019[10]). Table 3.2 outlines examples of activities that can be included in seven classes under CReMA.

Table 3.2. Classes under CReMA and examples of activities

Class	Examples of activities included in the class
CReMA10 Management of water	Minimisation of inland waters intake through in-process modifications Reduction of water losses and leaks or reduction of the intake by substituting the resource with alternative resources, water reuse and savings Restoration activities (recharge of groundwater bodies) Related activities/products for measurement, control, laboratories Related education, training and information and general administration activities
CReMA11 Management of forest resources	Restoration or replenishment activities or development of new forest areas Prevention and control of forest fires, diseases, pests and weeds, etc. Replacement or adjustment of production processes to reduce the input of forest-related products (wood and non-wood) Recovery, reuse or savings of forest products and by-products Related activities/products for measurement, control, laboratories Related education, training and information and general administration activities
CReMA12 Management of wild flora and fauna	Minimisation of the intake of wild flora and fauna (wild growing forest products are excluded) through in-process modifications, as well as withdrawals reduction and regulation measures Restoration activities (e.g. replenishment of wild flora and fauna stocks) Related activities/products for measurement, control, laboratories Related education, training and information and general administration activities
CReMA13 Management of energy resources	Production of energy from renewable sources Heat/energy saving and management Minimisation of the intake of fossil resources for raw materials for uses other than energy production Related activities/products for measurement, control, laboratories Related education, training and information and general administration activities
CReMA14 Management of minerals	Minimisation of the intake of minerals through in-process modifications Reduction of scraps Recovery of mineral-based materials Production of substitute for minerals-based materials Related activities/products for measurement, control, laboratories Related education, training and information and general administration activities
CReMA15 Research and development activities for resource management	Research and development for renewable energy, for energy and minerals savings, for timber and other biological resources savings, etc.
CReMA16 Other resource management activities	General administration of natural resources General administration Environmental management systems.

Source: Adapted from (Eurostat, 2016[3]), https://ec.europa.eu/eurostat/documents/3859598/7700432/KS-GQ-16-008-EN-N.pdf/f4965221-2ef0-4926-b3de-28eb4a5faf47.

Kazakhstan's statistical form for investment actually includes certain classes that may relate to CReMA13 (management of energy resources). These categories are investments in renewable energy sources; energy-saving technologies and energy efficiency; and reduction of greenhouse gas emissions. The Kazakh statistical system does not seem to collect investment-related data on other resource management activities than CReMA13. Moreover, Kazakhstan's statistical form for current expenditures does not explicitly include any of the categories under CReMA.

While CReMA can potentially be useful for Kazakhstan to better measure green finance flows, it might entail some technical challenges. Indeed, implementation of data collection under CReMA has proven to be challenging even in EU countries since its adoption in 2008. One study on the feasibility of CReMA implementation in Germany, for instance, concludes "it is problematic to identify resource management products in existing statistical classifications" and "resource management activities cannot be sufficiently mapped" in the country (Federal Statistical Office of Germany, 2017[11]).

A lack of clarity on the ideal scope of the resources makes it difficult to define a number of resource management activities (Eurostat, 2018[9]). Experts also argue that some definitions may become obsolete quickly, and that certain products or activities mentioned in the definitions may lead to an unintended negative impact on the environment (e.g. production of biofuels may lead to forest resource depletion) (Federal Statistical Office of Germany, 2017[11]).

In another challenge, it is not clear whether some activities belong to environmental protection or resource management. For example, climate change activities may fall under both CEPA1 and CReMA13 (Eurostat, 2018[9]). Some guidance has been developed to help understand the line between resource management and environmental protection activities. Reporting entities in Kazakhstan could also use this guidance if requested to report on such activities. Annex 6 of the EGSS Accounts Manual, prepared by Eurostat, could also be useful. It provides operational rules for treatment of borderline cases under CEPA and CReMA. One such example is cleaner versus more resource-efficient transport and other equipment (Eurostat, 2018[9]).

If Kazakhstan's statistical system were to use CReMA, it could face many more such borderline cases than the handful of examples in the Eurostat EGSS manual. This might lead to issues with regard to complexity of reporting and comparability of reported data. As a result, it would require a more detailed guideline tailored for Kazakh entities. Annexes 4 and 5 of the Eurostat manual also provide definitions, explanations and examples of activities under both CEPA and CReMA (Eurostat, 2016[3]). In addition, the annexes describe activities excluded from environmental protection or resource management activities[2], which could serve as a useful base to start developing a Kazakhstan-specific guideline.

It remains an important research topic for Eurostat to enhance consistency in scope, concepts, definitions and classification groupings across different SEEA accounts, including environmental protection and resource management (Eurostat, 2018[12]). The government of Kazakhstan can benefit from following the future development of this research agenda. For instance, Eurostat proposes a framework for the integration of different accounts, including, but not limited to, Environmental Protection Expenditure Accounts and Resource Management Expenditure Accounts (Eurostat, 2018[12]).

EU taxonomy of sustainable economic activities

Kazakhstan needs to continue its work on definitions of activities eligible to be green or sustainable finance. In this way, it could improve the national statistical system and further clarify what statistical forms should measure as green finance flows. The Astana International Finance Centre has launched work in this area with the People's Republic of China (hereafter "China"). However, the country could benefit from following existing or emerging work on sustainable or green finance taxonomies in other jurisdictions, particularly in the European Union (EU). Kazakhstan could also gain a wealth of insights from taxonomy work in China, Canada, France, Japan, the Netherlands and the United Kingdom, among others.

The European Commission created the Technical Expert Group (TEG) on Sustainable Finance, which started the work on four key actions proposed in the Commission's Action Plan on Financing Sustainable Growth in July 2018. One key action is to develop an EU taxonomy of sustainable economic activities. This is meant to be a technically robust classification system at the EU-level to provide clarity on what is "green" or "sustainable" (HLEG, 2018[13]) (see also Annex 3.A for further details).

The EU taxonomy of sustainable economic activities would aim to encourage sustainable growth by enhancing clarity and understanding among industry, investors and governments about which economic activities are environmentally sustainable. The taxonomy would make it possible to "measure financial flows towards sustainable development priorities at the asset, portfolio, institutional, regional, national and European levels" (HLEG, 2018[13]). The taxonomy may serve as a basis for future standards and labels for sustainable financial products that provide sustainable capital flows.

The draft EU taxonomy proposal sets out the criteria for determining the environmental sustainability of an economic activity, in line with six environmental objectives as follows:

- climate change mitigation
- climate change adaptation
- sustainable use and protection of water and marine resources
- transition to a circular economy, waste prevention and recycling
- pollution prevention control
- protection of healthy ecosystems.

For each of the economic activities and corresponding NACE sector codes[3], the taxonomy aims to establish principles, methodologies, metrics and thresholds to assess their degree of environmental sustainability. As the overarching principle, the sustainable activity should make a substantial positive contribution to one of the six environmental objectives, while not significantly harming any of the other five.

The government of Kazakhstan should closely follow development of the EU taxonomy. It could help elaborate definitions of activities for environmental protection and green economy transition provided under the statistical forms and associated instructions. The taxonomy, once finalised, could fill some gaps in the Kazakh national statistical system. For example, it could include how to integrate certain types of activities such as climate change adaptation. It might also suggest how to operationalise the notion of "do no significant harm", which means avoiding any significant negative impacts of an activity on other environmental or social issues.

The EU Taxonomy of Sustainable Economic Activities could help the country clarify what should be reported as green or sustainable finance. Building on an informal annex to the EU High-Level Expert Group (HLEG) report and other studies, Table 3.3 could help the government better understand specific activities and complement the classes under CEPA. The Committee on Statistics could use these classes to refine definitions of environmental protection and resource management activities, or develop new definitions where needed.

Table 3.3. Examples of climate change mitigation and adaptation activities

Sector	Climate change mitigation	Climate change adaptation
Energy	Renewable energy power plants Substantial GHG savings for fossil fuel power plants Biofuels Efficient district heating/cooling systems Electricity transmission and distribution Electricity storage Carbon capture and storage	Fortification of flood-prone energy infrastructure Minimised cooling water requirement Installation of water pumping back-up systems Modification of infrastructure siting during renovations or while planning new developments Micro-grids and distributed generation Back-up plans to provide for a rapid recovery from supply interruptions
Industry	Resource-efficient products, equipment and appliances Efficient fuel production facilities Efficient product manufacturing facilities Efficient storage and distribution Efficient retail outlets	Better siting of factories Greater resilience of industrial buildings, facilities and infrastructure to (e.g.) heavier rains Climate risk assessment to improve supply chain risk management
Building and urban planning	Energy-efficient buildings Low-carbon urban planning Low-carbon urban infrastructure	Reform of building codes and design standards House insurance Incentives for relocation
Transport	Low-carbon rail, road, air, and/or water transport systems Fuel switching	Updates of design and construction standards and materials in transport infrastructure Modification to transport asset management practice based on climate event Climate risk mapping of transport infrastructure
Water supply and management	Energy-efficient water supply and distribution Energy-efficient water treatment plants (incl. desalination)	Water conservation measures and effective water use

Sector	Climate change mitigation	Climate change adaptation
	Watershed management Water storage	Water storage, water demand management and technological development Safe drinking water and sanitation facilities during extreme events Movement of assets out of flood zones
Wastewater treatment	Wastewater treatment plants and sewage networks that contribute to energy saving or GHG emission avoidance	Direct and indirect reuse of treated wastewater
Waste management	Waste collection, sorting and materials recovery facilities Recycling Waste treatment that contributes to energy saving or GHG emission avoidance	Strengthened capacity of landfills, dumpsites and collection systems to combat natural disasters
Agriculture and fisheries	Climate-smart agriculture and husbandry Climate-smart fisheries and aquaculture	Development and use of crops more resilient to climate change Supplemental irrigation, intercropping systems, drip irrigation, levelling, etc. Management of pest or disease outbreaks Climate-resilient pasture and livestock management Climate-resilient horse production Crop insurance
Forestry	Reforestation and afforestation Plantations Management of forest fires	Management of forest fires Sustainable forestry and agro-forestry
Ecosystem	Conservation, restoration and enhancement of natural land habitats Restoration of degraded land	Development and use of saplings more resilient to climate change extremes and change Supplemental irrigation, drip irrigation Management of pest or disease outbreaks Ecosystem flood and/or storm damage protection Establishment of core protected areas and buffer zones Increased river dredging programmes Reinforcement of levees Re-establishment of natural flood plains and vegetation in upstream areas or riverbanks Management of pest or disease outbreaks Management of forest fires Degraded land restoration
Information and communication technology	Networks and communication facilities Information management system	Weather forecasting technologies Weather and climate services and information provision
Cross-cutting	Technical support and capacity building Research and development Public policy development Disaster relief products and services	More robust resilience programmes and improved enforcement Disaster risk plans and preparedness Development of revised codes for all design and operation of assets in all sectors, that consider climate change risks and require asset owners and managers to do so Research and development on climate-resilient crops.

Sources: Adapted from (KEPSA, 2014[14]), https://cdkn.org/wp-content/uploads/2015/04/Climate-Change-and-the-Energy-Sector.pdf;
(HLEG, 2018[15]), https://ec.europa.eu/info/sites/info/files/180131-sustainable-finance-final-report-annex-3_en.pdf;
(IEA, 2015[16]), https://webstore.iea.org/making-the-energy-sector-more-resilient-to-climate-change;
(Mavropoulos, 2011[17]), https://wastelessfuture.com/urban-waste-management-and-climate-change-adaptation/;
(Quium, 2015[18]), http://www.uncrd.or.jp/content/documents/345702_Abdul_Quium_Presentation_Kathmandu_Final.pdf;
(UNECE, 2014[19]), http://www.unece.org/env/water/.

In December 2018, the European Commission published a "Taxonomy Pack for Feedback". It invited technical experts and stakeholders to give feedback on selected economic activities and the proposed criteria for the first sub-set of economic activities for climate mitigation by February 2019. Ultimately, 244 respondents provided their feedback (TEG, 2018[6]).

As of March 2019, the taxonomy sub-group of the TEG was developing new criteria for the second round of climate change mitigation and adaptation activities, and "do no significant harm" assessment. The process was due to be completed in April 2019. The TEG planned to submit its final report to the European Commission in 2019. The report would include an explanation of how sectors were selected, and how technical screening criteria were determined in compliance with the taxonomy proposal. It would also analyse potential economic, financial and environmental impacts.

> **Box 3.1. Development of a green finance taxonomy by the Astana International Financial Centre**
>
> In Kazakhstan, the Astana International Financial Centre (AIFC) began developing the taxonomy of green finance for Kazakhstan in early 2019. The AIFC has already adopted the criteria on green bonds as part of the Rule Book of the Astana International Exchange. These criteria drew on the Green Bond Principles by the International Capital Market Association and the Climate Bonds Taxonomy of the Climate Bonds Standard (AIX, 2019[20]).
>
> A Kazakhstan-specific green finance taxonomy would be useful to complement government efforts to further refine or develop the definitions of activities for the country's green economy transition. One key objective of developing the taxonomy is indeed to help measure and report the flows and environmental impact of green projects (Ma, 2019[2]). Other objectives include:
>
> - providing financial institutions, businesses, policy makers and other market players with a common understanding and approach to identify, develop and finance green projects
> - increasing investors' confidence to finance green projects and reducing the risk of "greenwashing"
> - providing a basis for policy and regulatory incentives for green finance (Ma, 2019[2]).
>
> Sources: (AIX, 2019[20]), https://www.aix.kz/wp-content/uploads/2019/03/Green-Bonds-Rules.pdf; (Ma, 2019[2]).

OECD work on Environmental Protection Expenditure and Revenues (EPER)

OECD member countries have long reported on EPER as part of the OECD questionnaire on the state of the environment (OECD, 2014[4]). Countries use this questionnaire to gather the best available environmental data and promote international harmonisation of these data.

In 2016, the OECD Working Party on Environmental Information (WPEI) agreed to review the EPER section of the questionnaire. It aimed to align this section with SEEA and the framework used for EPEA. At the same time, the review also aimed at:

- finding ways to improve the quality of the data provided by countries
- exploring options to better cover expenditure in areas such as biodiversity, climate, and water supply.

The WPEI noted that climate change and biodiversity expenditure accounts would also be useful. However, with respect to climate change, it also noted that CEPA can only capture mitigation and not adaptation. The WPEI was requested to agree on the final version of the revised questionnaire (content, priority variables and terminology) by October 2019. This was to also include a decision on how to better cover expenditure in areas such as biodiversity, climate and water supply.

The government of Kazakhstan participated in the pilot testing of the OECD statistical questionnaire for EPER in 2018. This should become a practical step to improving Kazakhstan's statistical forms on current and investment expenditures for environmental protection. The exchanges held and feedback obtained through the pilot testing can be particularly useful in three areas. Specifically, they can further clarify activities to be included or excluded; improve usability of the statistical forms in Kazakhstan; and enhance quality and comparability of the relevant data.

Research collaborative on tracking finance for climate action

The OECD leads an open network called the Research Collaborative on Tracking Finance for Climate Action. It contributes towards data and methodological developments for tracking climate-related finance. The Research Collaborative co-ordinates governments, research organisations, development finance institutions, inter-governmental organisations and other relevant entities. It aims to share best available data, expertise and information to advance policy-relevant research on tracking climate finance in a comprehensive and timely manner (See (OECD, n.d.[5])for further information).

In light of tracking progress in relation to Article 2.1c of the Paris Agreement, the Research Collaborative initiated country-level pilot studies. These aim to track financial flows into new infrastructure and equipment, as well as refurbishment of existing ones. They combine different sources of financial data, complemented with estimates based on non-financial proxies (Dobrinevski and Jachnik, 2019[21]).

In the medium- to long-term, Kazakhstan might benefit from the methodologies developed by the Research Collaborative and outcomes of its country-level studies on tracking finance flows to help assess their consistency with climate objectives. These could particularly help Kazakhstan improve data quality and explore data that are more granular by sector or sub-sector, type of technology, financial instrument and provider of finance, among others. Such work would also help the government assess finance flows that contribute to climate objectives. Furthermore, they could identify financial flows to activities that undermine its climate change objectives, evaluate effectiveness of policies in shifting finance for low-carbon and climate-resilient investment, and complement non-financial indicators on climate mitigation (Jachnik, Mirabile and Dobrinevski, 2019[22]).

Climate Public Expenditures and Institutional Review by UNDP

Another example that could help improve the Kazakh statistical system, especially on public expenditure, would be the Climate Public Expenditures and Institutional Review (CPEIR) led by the United Nations Development Programme (UNDP). CPEIR is a systematic qualitative and quantitative analysis of public expenditures by different ministries of a country. It aims to improve how those different streams of public expenditures relate to climate change objectives (UNDP, 2015[7]). CPEIRs have been conducted in 17 countries (UNDP, n.d.[23]). CPEIR consists of three pillars:

1. **Policy analysis**: a review of the climate change policy framework and its monitoring framework, as well as how the policy objectives translate into programmes and instruments;
2. **Institutional analysis**: an analysis of the roles and responsibilities of institutions and their capacities in formulating, implementing and co-ordinating climate responses;
3. **Climate public expenditure analysis**: a quantification of climate-relevant expenditure out of the total national budget and measure.

Climate public expenditure analysis starts with collecting data and deciding whether expenditure items are climate-relevant. The next step is to classify the climate-related expenditures. The UNDP's guidelines on CPEIR outline multiple approaches to classification, such as Standardised UNDP/World Bank CPEIR Typology and the National Policy Objectives Typology. Once climate-related expenditures are classified, the weight of climate relevance to these expenditures can be applied to assess the proportion related to climate change (UNDP, 2015[7]).

Some activities primarily target climate change mitigation or adaptation, or both, while others may have climate-related components as a secondary objective. The CPEIR guidebook outlines two approaches to applying the weight to each expenditure depending on the relevance to climate change: the Climate Relevance Index and the Benefit Cost Ratio. These two approaches are not mutually exclusive and the decision of which one to use would depend on the level of data available for the analysis (UNDP, 2015[7]).

Implications for further improvement in Kazakhstan's national statistical system

The joint work by the Committee on Statistics and the OECD on the SEEA coherence has concluded that Kazakhstan's statistics on investment and current (operational) expenditures for environmental protection is appropriately structured and aligned with good international practice as in CEPA (OECD, 2019[8]). Existing data under the national statistical system are similar in structure and detail to the EPEA compiled by EU member states that is also based also on CEPA. However, they do not yet completely adhere to EPEA (Eurostat, n.d.[24]).

A greater level of alignment between Kazakhstan's statistical system and the SEEA should provide insights into how to enhance granularity of the data. This could include, for example, disaggregated expenditure data into environmental protection-specific services, connected products, adapted goods and capital formation. This could be further enhanced through Kazakhstan's ongoing participation in pilot testing for the revised statistical questionnaire for the EPER, implemented under the OECD WPEI.

While this study does not recommend immediate, fully-fledged application of CReMA to the Kazakh system, future use could further clarify types of resource management activities for consideration. For instance, the use of CReMA could refine definitions of activities for energy saving and production of energy by renewable sources, which have already been covered by the statistical form for investment. It could also help Kazakhstan decide which sectors should receive more coverage, such as measures for efficient use of water, forest or mineral resources. The Committee on Statistics could consider gradual adoption of those CReMA classes that could be particularly relevant to the green economy transition of Kazakhstan. To that end, it could follow closely the EU's work under the European Strategy for Environmental Accounts 2019-23.

The EU Taxonomy of Sustainable Economic Activities, once finalised, could also complement Kazakhstan's effort to further elaborate the definitions of green economy activities in different policy domains. These include areas such as climate change adaptation and mitigation, biodiversity, circular economy and air pollution, among others. The taxonomy could also provide some more considerations on how to operationalise the notions of "do no significant harm", to avoid any significant negative impacts of an activity on other environmental or social issues.

Development of a Kazakh Green Finance Taxonomy by the Astana International Finance Centre should also inform development of methodologies for green finance measurement. Efforts to develop such a Kazakh-specific taxonomy should be aligned with the development of the EU taxonomy, as well as with other national-level sustainable finance taxonomies that already exist or are under development. This could also be complemented by the UNDP's typologies for the Climate Public Expenditures and Institutional Reviews.

The country-level work by the Research Collaborative could also help the Committee on Statistics explore methodologies to tracking finance with further details over the long term. For instance, Research Collaborative work might inform potential future work by the Committee on Statistics on how to obtain disaggregated data by sector or sub-sector, type of technology, financial instrument and provider of finance, among others. In particular, the statistical system does not clearly capture green finance flows to households or as part of foreign direct investment (FDI). Collecting "green" FDI would require closer co-ordination with the National Bank of Kazakhstan since it is in charge of collecting FDI data in general.

Annex 3.A. The European Commission's Action Plan on Financing Sustainable Growth

In March 2018, the Financial Stability and Capital Markets Directorate of the European Commission (EC) launched a broad Action Plan on Financing Sustainable Growth. In May 2018, it proposed a legislative package to implement its action plan. This package was based on recommendations of the industry-led EU High-Level Expert Group (HLEG) on Sustainable Finance in January 2018, following a collaborative and inclusive process in 2017 and 2018. The three objectives of the action plan are:

1. Reorient capital flows towards sustainable investment to achieve sustainable and inclusive growth;
2. Manage financial risks stemming from climate, environmental degradation and social issues;
3. Foster transparency and long-termism in financial and economic activity.

In May 2018, the EC adopted three legislative proposals to start implementing its action plan. It proposed two regulations to facilitate sustainable investment and for disclosures relating to sustainable investments and sustainability risks. It also proposed a new category of stock market benchmarks. In June 2018, the EC set up a Technical Expert Group (TEG) on sustainable finance to help develop the delegated acts that will follow adoption of the above draft legislations.

The sustainable finance taxonomy proposal of the European Commission

The draft legislation aims to identify which economic activities can be defined as "environmentally sustainable" as per EU legislation. The economic activities are based on the Statistical Classification of Economic Activities in the European Community used by the EC. "Environmental sustainability" is based on six environmental objectives: climate change adaptation, climate change mitigation, water use, waste and recycling, pollution and protection of ecosystems.

To qualify as "environmentally sustainable", an economic activity will need to contribute substantially to one of six environmental objectives and "do no significant harm" to the five other objectives. Notably, the use of the taxonomy will be mandatory only for investors wishing to refer to the "sustainability" of activities as per EC legislation.

The development of the full-fledged taxonomy will span several years. The first version will focus on economic activities identified as priorities for climate adaptation and mitigation, including minimum social standards. Further elaboration will detail criteria for a larger "environmental taxonomy", as well as social and governance criteria. The taxonomy will be adaptable and will evolve over time, considering the development of technologies. The TEG on sustainable finance (including the OECD, which is serving as an observer), has led a consultation process with external experts. The aim is to devise principles, methodologies and technical screening criteria (e.g. emissions thresholds) for qualification for a number of priority activities and for the six objectives.

The legislative process

The relevant Committees of European Parliament voted on the taxonomy (based on proposed amendments to the legislative proposal below) on 28 March 2019. The TEG was tasked to draft a report and submit recommendations for public consultation during the summer of 2019. The TEG's mission was expected to terminate at the end of 2019. Further information may be available (TEG, 2018[25]).

References

AIX (2019), *AIX Green Bonds Rules*, Astana International Exchange, Nur-Sultan, https://www.aix.kz/wp-content/uploads/2019/03/Green-Bonds-Rules.pdf. [20]

Dobrinevski, A. and R. Jachnik (2019), "Tracking finance flows and investment needs for the energy and climate transition: Tracking finance flows in the context of Article 2.1c of the Paris Agreement", presentation at the tracking finance flows and investment needs for the energy and climate transition conference, Berlin, March, http://wise-europa.eu/wp-content/uploads/2019/03/Session3_Tracking-finance-flows-in-the-context-of-Article-2.1c-of-the-Paris-Agreement-_OECD-2.pdf. [21]

European Statistical System Committee (2019), *39 th Meeting of the European Statistical System Committee*, https://ec.europa.eu/eurostat/documents/1798247/6191525/European+Strategy+for+Environmental+Accounts/ (accessed on 24 April 2019). [10]

EuroStat (2018), *Environmental protection expenditure accounts: National expenditure on environmental protection 2006-2017*, https://ec.europa.eu/eurostat/statistics-explained/index.php?title=Environmental_protection_expenditure_accounts#General_overview (accessed on 11 February 2019). [26]

Eurostat (2018), "Classification of environmental activities", presentation at the London Group on Environmental Accounting, Dublin, October, https://seea.un.org/sites/seea.un.org/files/lg_24_b_7.pdf. [9]

Eurostat (2018), *Integrated framework for environmental activity accounts*, Directorate E: Sectoral and regional statistics Unit E-2: Environmental statistics and accounts; sustainable development, Statistical Office of the European Union, Brussels, https://seea.un.org/sites/seea.un.org/files/seea_paper_integrated_framework_estat_v5.pdf. [12]

Eurostat (2016), *Environmental Goods and Services Sector Accounts Manual: 2016 Edition*, Statistical Office of the European Union, Brussels, https://ec.europa.eu/eurostat/documents/3859598/7700432/KS-GQ-16-008-EN-N.pdf/f4965221-2ef0-4926-b3de-28eb4a5faf47 (accessed on 11 January 2019). [3]

Eurostat (n.d.), "Environmental Protection Expenditure", (database), Statistical Office of the European Union (Accessed on 21 March 2019), https://ec.europa.eu/eurostat/web/environment/environmental-protection-expenditure. [24]

Federal Statistical Office of Germany (2017), *Feasibility study on reporting under the Classification of Resource Management Activities (CReMA) and on Resource Management Expenditure Accounts (ReMEA) according to the new modules of Regulation 691/2011*, https://www.destatis.de/EN/Methods/MethodologicalPapers/Download/FeasibilityStudySchlesag.pdf?__blob=publicationFile. [11]

HLEG (2018), *Financing a Sustainable European Economy: Final Report 2018 by the High-Level Expert Group on Sustainable Finance - Secretariat provided by the European Commission*, High-Level Expert Group on Sustainable Finance, Brussels, https://ec.europa.eu/info/sites/info/files/180131-sustainable-finance-final-report_en.pdf. [13]

HLEG (2018), *Informal supplementary document on sustainable taxonomy (Annex III to the Final report of the High-Level Expert Group on Sustainable Finance)*, High-Level Expert Group on Sustainable Finance, Brussels, https://ec.europa.eu/info/sites/info/files/180131-sustainable-finance-final-report-annex-3_en.pdf. [15]

IEA (2015), "Making the Energy Sector More Resilient to Climate Change", International Energy Agency, Paris, https://webstore.iea.org/making-the-energy-sector-more-resilient-to-climate-change. [16]

Jachnik, R., M. Mirabile and A. Dobrinevski (2019), "Tracking finance flows towards assessing their consistency with climate objectives", *OECD Environment Working Papers*, No. 146, OECD Publishing, Paris, https://dx.doi.org/10.1787/82cc3a4c-en. [22]

KEPSA (2014), *Climate Change and the Energy and Manufacturing Sector*, Climate Change and Your Business Briefing Note Series, April, Kenya Private Sector Alliance, Nairobi, https://cdkn.org/wp-content/uploads/2015/04/Climate-Change-and-the-Energy-Sector.pdf. [14]

Ma, J. (2019), "Green finance and green taxonomies", presentation at the AIFC workshop on green taxonomy, Nur-Sultan, April. [2]

Mavropoulos, A. (2011), *Urban waste management and climate change adaptation*, Wasteless Future Blog, https://wastelessfuture.com/urban-waste-management-and-climate-change-adaptation/ (accessed on 10 April 2019). [17]

OECD (2019), *Agreement between the government of the Republic of Kazakhstan and the Organisation for Economic Co-operation and Development for the realisation of the project "Implementation of the System of Environmental Economic Accounting": Interim Report*, OECD, Paris. [8]

OECD (2016), *Kazakhstan GREEN Action Platform*, http://www.oecd.org/env/outreach/kazakhstangreenactionplatform.htm (accessed on 16 January 2019). [1]

OECD (2014), *Questionnaire on the State of the Environment*, https://www.oecd.org/statistics/data-collection/Environmental%20Data_SOE%20guidelines.pdf (accessed on 6 January 2020). [4]

OECD (n.d.), *Research Collaborative on Tracking Private Climate Finance*, https://www.oecd.org/env/researchcollaborative/ (accessed on 25 April 2019). [5]

Quium, A. (2015), "Transport infrastructure – Adaptation to climate change and extreme weather impacts", presentation at regional seminar on Safe, Climate Adaptive and Disaster Resilient Transport for Sustainable Development, Kathmandu, November, http://www.uncrd.or.jp/content/documents/345702_Abdul_Quium_Presentation_Kathmandu_Final.pdf. [18]

TEG (2018), *Spotlight on Taxonomy*, Technical Expert Group on Sustainable Finance of the European Commission, Brussels, http://ec.europa.eu/transparency/regdoc/rep/1/2018/EN/COM-2018-353-F1-EN-MAIN-PART-1.PDF. [25]

TEG (2018), *Taxonomy pack for feedback and workshops invitations December 2019*, Technical Expert Group on Sustainable Finance, Brussels, https://ec.europa.eu/info/sites/info/files/business_economy_euro/banking_and_finance/documents/sustainable-finance-taxonomy-feedback-and-workshops_en.pdf. [6]

UNDP (2015), *A Methodological Guidebook: Climate Public Expenditure and Institutional Review (CPEIR)*, UNDP Bangkok Regional Hub, http://www.asia-pacific.undp.org/content/rbap/en/home/library/democratic_governance/cpeir-methodological-guidebook.html. [7]

UNDP (n.d.), *CPEIR Country Database | Governance of Climate Change Finance for Asia-Pacific*, https://www.climatefinance-developmenteffectiveness.org/CPEIR-Database (accessed on 10 January 2019). [23]

UNECE (2014), *Guidance on Water and Adaptation to Climate Change*, Water Convention, http://www.unece.org/env/water/ (accessed on 25 April 2019). [19]

Notes

[1] Connected products are those whose use directly serves environmental protection purposes, but which are not species services related to environmental protection or inputs into characteristic activities. Adapted goods are goods that have been specifically modified to be more "environmentally friendly" or "cleaner" and whose use is therefore beneficial for environmental protection. Examples of adapted goods include de-sulphurised fuels, mercury-free batteries and CFC-free products.

[2] In terms of developing the national accounts for environmental goods and services, a challenge is to identify "borderline cases" between CEPA and CReMA (see page 24 of Eurostat 2016). However, for the purpose of tracking green finance within the country, there are two additional more important challenges. First, Kazakhstan must avoid "double counting" (where the same expense is reported twice in different classes) in the total finance flows. Second, it must ensure that reporting entities understand which activities should be categorised in which classes in a consistent manner.

[3] NACE : Nomenclature statistique des activités économiques dans la Communauté européenne. For more information, see : https://ec.europa.eu/eurostat/statistics-explained/index.php/Glossary:Statistical_classification_of_economic_activities_in_the_European_Community_(NACE)

www.ingramcontent.com/pod-product-compliance
Lightning Source LLC
LaVergne TN
LVHW061949070526
838199LV00060B/4040